Barkingside

Memories

Barkingside

Memories

Helen Finch

TEMPUS

Frontispiece: Fairlop Oak public house outing, c. 1949.

First published 2005

Tempus Publishing Limited
The Mill, Brimscombe Port,
Stroud, Gloucestershire, GL5 2QG
www.tempus-publishing.com

British Library Cataloguing in Publication Data.
A catalogue record for this book is available from the British Library.

ISBN 0 7524 3517 5

Typesetting and origination by Tempus Publishing Limited.
Printed in Great Britain.

Contents

Acknowledgements 6

Introduction 7

one Early Memories 9

two Schooldays and Growing up 21

three All in a Day's Work 37

four Leisure and Pastimes 51

five Wartime Experiences 63

six Home Life 73

seven The High Street 83

eight Here and There 91

nine Village Life 103

ten Memorable Times 113

Acknowledgements

Special thanks go to my family, especially my husband Roy and my son Thomas who have been very patient with me. Also to our new addition, Luke, who slept at the appropriate times. To my mother who 'spread the word' about this publication. To Cranley Calendars; William Torbitt School website; Dr Barnardo's Homes, Barkingside (Christopher Reeve); Redbridge Public Libraries, Local History Section; Recorder Newspapers; Gazette Newspapers; Brian and Joyce Piggott (for loan of photographs); and Peter Aitken-Smith and Stokely Volney for their technical expertise.

Thanks are also extended to the numerous contributors who appear in this book, for sparing me their time, precious memories, photographs and personal items. Without these my vision of a local oral history book would not have been possible. I also thank anyone else who has helped at any stage of this publication even if you haven't been mentioned by name.

Last but not least, I would like to thank various members of Brentwood Writers Group who have supported, inspired and given me the courage to complete such a task, and my cousin, Joanna Wilkins, whose historical knowledge encouraged me to pursue this venture and brought both family and local history to life.

Every effort has been made to obtain permission for photographs where necessary but I apologise if anyone has been overlooked. The facts in this book to my knowledge are correct, bearing in mind they are from memory. Please accept my apologies, however, for any errors or omissions.

Introduction

The 'Barking' side of the forest. This is how Barkingside is described in historical literature. Once a small village situated approximately five miles from Barking and three miles from Ilford, Barkingside has grown into a very populated town in its own right, despite many still confusing it with Barking. Many local names have stuck, including Gaysham Hall, which is now flats, although once a large working estate. Claybury is now known as Repton Park although locals will still call it by its original name.

Although Barkingside does not boast the vast array of shops that adorn nearby Ilford and Romford, it does have a variety of stores for everyday needs – some would argue that this was the case even more so, many years before. Redbridge Magistrates Court and Tesco stores now replace some of Dr Barnardo's Village and you will notice as you read the memories how the shops have changed hands more rapidly as time has progressed. The police station was once a little further along the Cranbrook Road and when extended some time ago, replaced some quaint cottages that were next to the Recreation Ground.

Having a varied public transport system and close to main road networks has made Barkingside and the surrounding areas easily accessible for travel; thus now we see more movement of residents from inner cities out to the 'country'.

Larger buildings and residences have replaced small village shops and homes. Unfortunately this has resulted in the loss of open farmland and fields that were once held at a very high price for many of the landowners and locals whose relatives worked them for a living. Some reminders of time past still thankfully live on. Cottages can be seen in various places, some of the remaining public houses, despite having been refurbished several times, are generally the same, and for a quiet moment you could be transported back to a time when horse and carts, trams and rationing was an integral part of life.

Dr Barnardo chose Barkingside and Woodford Bridge as sites for his Village Homes, affording cleaner air than that in London. Some of the village in Barkingside still remains (although now occupied by offices) along with Barnardo's village church, a towering shadow over Tanners Lane.

Travelling down Forest Road you can almost imagine the planes flying over and the ack-ack guns reverberating in the sky. Having seen action in both world wars as Fairlop Airfield we are lucky to have retained these areas as open spaces on both sides of the road.

The Claybury Tower is still an intimidating sight, noticeable for miles around. On a clear day from a high point in Hainault Forest looking down Forest Road, one can see London in the distance, reminding us of the London Borough status. The proposed racecourse at Fairlop Waters will bring again more change, making me wonder what previous generations would have made of it.

Local people are commemorated. William Ingram, a local builder of Pert Cottages in Tanners Lane, has a stained glass window in Holy Trinity church and is buried there in the churchyard with other members of his family. William Torbitt, of the Newbury Park school bearing his name, has only recently had a memorial headstone erected in his honour at Barkingside cemetery, attended by ex-pupils and members of his family.

Within these pages are not just memories of Barkingside but also the surrounding area. Many excursions were taken to slightly outlying places as well as residents from these areas, such as Aldborough Hatch, Chigwell Row and Hainault, travelling to Barkingside to shop.

Being a 'Barkingsider' as were my ancestors before, I feel it is important to record the fascinating stories of local people, some of whom still live in the area, some that have moved away. Oral history plays a major part in capturing the past for future generations, offering an understanding of local and social history. It has been my pleasure to delve into the memories of the people and their families, both past and present, for this book; memories of schooldays, hobbies and entertainment. We also hear how religion played a part in family life. Disruptions through wartime that would inconvenience most of society today brought people closer together. The message that cries out from the pages is that the past is something to cherish. This publication has given the chance for contributors to do this for others to enjoy.

I thoroughly enjoyed meeting the contributors and collecting the material for the book, so it is to them that I dedicate this work. Without them sparing me the time and their precious photographs it would not have been possible.

Helen Finch
February, 2005

one

Early Memories

Honesty and Hoover bags

I remember being brought up so honest that one day after buying some Hoover bags in the local shops in Hainault, I returned home to find that although I had paid for one set of bags, I had two as they were stuck together. I was mortified and promptly walked all the way back to the shop to tell them. I wonder how many people in this day and age would be that honest?

Amanda Ross

Collapsible seats

I was born in Thundersley, but my earliest memory of Barkingside was walking along the High Street to catch a tram, which was down by the Chequers, and travelling along Ley Street with my father to Ilford. The things that most amazed me about it was that they had wooden seats and if the tram was going one way the seats would be one way, and when it came for the tram to come back they would turn the seats around the other way. They were just pushed back and collapsible and you would always be facing forwards. My husband said that they used to put the mail on the front of the

Trolleybus No. 691 to Barkingside, 1940s.

trams and that would be taken into Ilford. The trams finished before the war, probably about 1936/37. But then the trolleybuses came and that is when they built the roundabout because they had to have the trolleybuses going round and back again down the High Street.

Irene Vaughan

Fishy thoughts

There were not many small boys who loved to go into Gurr's fish shop, but I did. It was a wet fish shop, although they did some fish and chips in a separate small building at the back, reached down the small alley at the side of the shop. They also sold some meat, if I recall, especially near Christmas when the left-hand side of the shop was devoted to turkeys and chickens. My dad always got our Christmas turkey from Gurr's, insisting that their quality was always superior to other butcher's shops. When you bought your fish, the shop assistant that served you would produce a small, wet, fish-smelling piece of paper with your bill on it, you would take it to the lady in the pay booth at the end of the shop and pay for your purchases. I remember the sight of the fish laid out on ice and the distinctive fish smell. I wonder why that held such an allure for me?

Derek Lawrence

Katherine Gardens

I lived in Katherine Gardens from 1948 to 1969. It was still very rural there. At the end of Katherine Gardens were fields, one of which had been bombed leaving a large crater which seemed permanently full of water. I remember it icing over in the winter. Going up Fencepiece Road towards Chigwell there was the United Dairy depot and horses were still being used. Limes Farm had many fields along Fencepiece Road and at the top were riding stables.

Faye Pedder

Sleepy subway

I was born in Newbury Park in 1933. My parents had moved from London out to the country area. Just before the war, bunks were put in the subway outside William Torbitt School. I remember walking through the subway as a child and being very frightened. I thought people would still be there asleep.

Ron Jeffries

Checking the house

I was born in 1940 and my parents brought a house in Craven Gardens. Not long after, my father went off to India during the Second World War and I moved with my mother to live with my Nan and Granddad in Windsor Road, Ilford. My mum went back to our house every weekend to make sure it was still standing. I was five when my father came home and unfortunately I treated him like a stranger. We moved back to Barkingside then. My father was also very strict and I wasn't allowed to go to the pictures on a Sunday, although I went on Saturday mornings and took my brother.

Ron Jeffries, 2005.

Over the back to where we lived were allotments and I would go and pick rhubarb. You could walk right through from the roundabout to Barkingside station. We would go up the hill at the station and there were bits of metal you could sit on and slide down. The gun turrets were down at the bottom.

Ann Reed (*née* Croft)

Tomswood Hill, 1930s

There were very few houses apart from the council houses and cottages in Tomswood Hill. Colvin Gardens was not built until about 1931/2. On the corner of Mossford Lane was Cooper's Nursery where one could purchase tomatoes etc., and further down attached to a cottage was a small sweet shop called Burgess. At the back of it were tennis courts.

M. Ellis

Bayko bricks

I remember playing with my doll's house, Bayko building bricks (probably now con-demned on the grounds of health and safety), doing jigsaws and playing board games. However, my greatest love was reading and my mother remembers me sitting in the apple tree at the end of our garden reading.

E. Wood

Father Christmas

One freezing cold night when I was about three years old, I was sitting in our Anderson shelter with my mother, great aunt and Mr Rice the watchmaker when a policeman suddenly appeared at the doorway and spoke to my mother. He looked frozen and was clap-ping his hands together to warm himself. My mother invited him in and gave him a cup of hot tea which she poured from a tin jug with a lid on it. He looked so old, just like Father Christmas.

V. Payne

Move to Aldborough Hatch

My parents and I moved to the Aldborough Stores off-licence, Aldborough Road North, Newbury Park, in 1955 and lived there until 1965. I was five when we arrived and I joined the infants of the William Torbitt School that was opposite the shop. I stayed at this school until I was eleven and then went on to what was Ilford County High School for Girls (now Valentines High) at Gants Hill.

Brenda Graisgour

Walk to Barkingside

My family didn't have a car so we walked, bussed or took the train everywhere. We lived on the edge of the Hainault estate, near Manford Way, nearer to Grange Hill. When I was very young, before the Manford Way shops were built, we either walked to Grange Hill or Hainault to shop. Once a week we did a big shop in Barkingside. My mother would push my younger brother Colin in a pushchair and if I got tired I was allowed to stand on the footboard. When we passed Hainault station mother would let us stop and look in the tall case that was outside Townsend Jewellers. It had the most incredible animated clocks I have ever seen, even until this day.

Patricia Lange (*née* Dawson)

Christening of Pancake Hill

When my late husband was younger and Barkingside was mostly fields, he and his friends would play over in the Claybury fields where there were lots of cattle. One particular time he was running about and slipped in a cowpat, sliding down the hill and making a

Right: Mr and Mrs Croft with baby Ann in 1940.

Below: Gresham cottages, Tomswood Hill built in the 1800s, still standing today.

mess of his trousers. Needless to say his mother wasn't best pleased. However, one thing did come out of it, that part of the Claybury estate was christened 'Pancake Hill'.

E. Kemble

Dad's early life

My father was born at Great Gales Farm, Woodford Bridge. The family then moved down to Forest Farm, Forest Road, in the end house. He inscribed his name on the end of the wall. In recent years, after he came out of the army, he was talking to a chap, telling him he used to live there and asked whether he had noticed a brick inscribed with 'CB Winter' on it and he said that he had. My father would walk from there to Trinity school and one of his mates at school was Reg Lee who used to run the flower carry on. In his teenage years he had an uncle who had a farm up at Grange Hill. He always called it Winter's Farm but I don't know how true this was. After this, when he was sixteen years old he joined the army and became a boy soldier.

Charles Ernest Winter

Edmonton to Barkingside – what a contrast!

We had moved to Barkingside from Edmonton at the beginning of 1935. My father had taken a job as foreman carpenter at a small wood yard and factory in New North Road. The house was attached to the factory building on one side and surrounded by the wood yard on the other side and back, and although there was a fairly large garden it faced the main road. A complete difference from the row of small cottages, fields and a road that barred entry to traffic that surrounded us in Edmonton. What there was of a garden at the back of the house was dwarfed by a large pear tree. Oh, how I remember the lovely sweet William pears.

Jean Westbeech (*née* Thompson)

Blackout

I hated the blackout; it made the room so oppressive. I have suffered from claustrophobia for as long as I can remember and think this originated from the bedroom I shared with my mother. The blackout was total and the bedroom door was closed. I would lie in the darkness feeling as though I couldn't breathe. One night my mother rushed into the room, jumped on the bed and pulled the pillow over our heads. There was a tremendous noise of bombing that seemed to go on and on. We lay there like that for a long time, I felt suffocated even though my mother talked to me constantly and told me stories. She must have got very worried because every now and again she would sing a hymn then say a prayer. I just wished I could take the pillow off.

V. Payne

Lighting up

Just a bit further, on the roundabout, was the light shop. If you were ever about when it was dark the crystal chandeliers would light up the roundabout. They sold small lamps shaped like toadstool houses and one could peep inside. Little china mice would be in a variety of poses, the glow from the lamp in the roof shone so it looked like their own houses with the light on. These were very expensive, along with most of the lights in the shop, so looking through the window was the only thing I did.

H. Kemble

House sharing

My parents managed to rent the ground floor of a house at No. 60 Birkbeck Road, Newbury Park, just round the corner from my mother's sister Grace. The upper floor was rented to a childless couple, Mr and Mrs Jacques. We had a kitchen with a back door to the garden, the

Forest Farm cottages, 2005.

dining room had a French door into a lean-to. In the dining room there was the dining table and four chairs, two armchairs, a sideboard and a piano. At one end of the lean-to was a galvanized coalbunker. The front room was the bedroom, shared by all four of us; one double bed, two cots and a wardrobe. Upstairs, I believe, the small bedroom was their kitchen and the other two upstairs rooms were their dining room and bedroom. Both families had to share the upstairs bathroom and toilet. We had a coal fire in both rooms but usually only the back one was used as coal was on ration. I remember my mother blacking the fire front with Zebo. If it was really cold in the winter my father used to take a shovelful of hot coals from the back room and use it to make a fire in the bedroom for us.

V.E. Bush

Scrumping

Beyond the green alleyway were the houses that backed onto the other side of Merlin Grove which came from Tomswood Hill. There was a big old house there which had loads of land and big orchards. We used to go scrumping and if we were caught we would get told off!

Linda Reside

Crown Road

I was six years old when our family moved from Gordon Road in Ilford to Crown Road in Barkingside. It was a new house and the area was expanding in 1926.

John Knight

Council house expansion

I was born in 1949 in the front bedroom of our council house, Waltham Road, Woodford

Left: V.E. Bush, 2005.

Below: Merlin Grove, *c*. 1962.

Opposite: The Pond and St Paul's church, Woodford Bridge.

Bridge. I was always told by my parents that I came along to help them get a house, as I already had a sister two years older than me and they were all living in a tiny flat in Wanstead. Being pregnant got them the 'points' they needed for a house. That's how it worked in those days. Plus the fact they wanted another baby anyway.

Joyce Piggott

Trip to the countryside

I was born in Ilford and have lived in Redbridge, as it is now known all of my life, apart from five-and-a-half years in the air force. I remember coming to Barkingside on the tram with my father when I was young. It was like a trip to the countryside. We moved to Barkingside in 1934 but moved to Seven Kings after my sister suddenly died. After the start of the Second World War my father died so we came back to live in Barkingside again.

Ron Ketteridge

Thursday ice cream

Every Thursday we had ice cream and we had to go across to the stores at Barnardo's with our dish. That was fine in the autumn and winter but in the summer, by the time you got them back to your cottage they were milk. The ice creams were round with a piece of paper wrapped at the bottom.

Kathy Alston

Dunspring Lane

My husband spent most of his childhood living in Dunspring Lane. His father owned the pharmacy in Claybury Broadway.

E. Wood

Fencepiece Evangelical church and St Francis of Assisi

I was asked on my first day to name a song to sing. I suggested 'Humpty Dumpty' and was most upset to be told that they only sang songs about Jesus. I also remember my nursery school. It was in the hall behind St Francis' church.

Amanda Ross

Dunspring Lane.

Who will be my partner?

We did country dancing at school and I remember one dance in particular, it was called 'The Idle Robin', don't ask me why. If there was a boy that you liked you could be lucky and get to dance with him but invariably you got the horrible one that had sweaty palms.

Linda Reside

Finding the right house

I moved to Barkingside with my parents in 1931. My Dad was a Ford worker and he was one of the first to come down from Manchester when Ford's factory opened up. He lived in Ilford a year before we did and he walked round and found this place in Fencepiece Road. It was a little country village then.

Roy Wilkinson

Arrived with a bang!

I was born on 24 October 1940. As the land mine landed, I popped into the world with the front door blowing off its hinges and all the windowpanes showering onto my three-year-old sister asleep in her cot.

Pat Owers (*née* Hunter)

The Chase

We would walk down The Chase which came up to Oaks Lane. This was a bridle path and would come round the other side of St Peter's church, Aldborough Hatch.

D. Williams

Ethel Gardens

I was born in Plaistow in 1925 and when I was about two years old we went to live at Ethel Gardens, Tomswood Hill. We had the two upstairs rooms in the house where Mum's friend lived with her new husband.

St Francis of Assisi and Fairlop Evangelical church, Fencepiece Road was built around 1960 and is seen here in 2005.

I remember Ethel Gardens as a row of fairly up-to-date conjoined two-storey houses opposite the grounds of Claybury Hospital. Hainault Forest was just up the road, and down the hill was a more built-up area on the way to the Maypole. At the back of our house were open fields and not far over was a disused well. Quite dangerous really – just a wooden cover you could lift off, there in the long grass. Other children living in Ethel Gardens were Winnie and Jack Howe and Gracie Mead. We moved to Hornchurch when I was about six.

Joan Medlock

Mrs Bliss

Mrs Bliss would come to the school pushing her pram and sit outside before it opened with all the halfpenny and farthing sweets. She lived in Fencepiece Road. If we were going up to school I would ask if I could push her pram and she would tell me that I was a good boy and give me a penny-worth of sweets. At the end of the day she would be there again and we would rush out to push her pram home.

Roy Wilkinson

Midwife praise

I was born in 1941 in Hitchen, Hertfordshire, at my grandparents house. When only a few weeks old we moved to Barkingside where I lived until my marriage in 1965, then moving to Romford. My brother was born at No. 18 Fencepiece Road in 1944 and my mother was praised one morning by the midwife for not getting up and going to the Anderson shelter after a particularly heavy raid the night before, as many of the other mothers had.

Alison Bush (*née* Dryborough)

Brandville Gardens

I went to Barkingside school in Mossford Green in the early 1920s and we lived in

Above left: Roy Wilkinson and his lorry in a field at the back of Fencepiece Road, 1954.

Above right: Linda Reside, 2005.

Brandville Gardens. They were built on Great Gearies which was the posh house on the main road. It has now been built on. I remember playing on the bricks as the new houses went up. The builder was Brand (named Brandville Gardens after him). The school was the only one in Barkingside at the side of the parish church of Holy Trinity. There was a stove in the centre and we had two classes, the lower class and the upper. There was a coke fire. Gearies was then built and I was one of the first pupils there. Barkingside was just being built up, becoming a suburb of London.

John Baker

Bilco

I was lucky that my dad worked at Truman's Brewery so we got lots of cheap fizzy drinks. I also remember the lemonade deliveryman from Bilco who drove round all the streets and sold pop in every flavour including limeade and cherryade.

Amanda Ross

Road safety

When I was in the infants' school the police used to come and lay out the playground with black and white poles like a road and they would teach you road safety such as where to cross. They would have people dressed as clowns to help you remember where to cross and they would act out an accident to show you what could happen if you didn't cross in the correct place.

Linda Reside

Hiding in the library

I was an avid reader and always went to the branch library at the far end of the High Street. I would walk down Tomswood after school, stopping at home to pick up some of my mother's bread pudding she had made. I would choose books and sit in a corner quietly reading and eating, making sure the librarian, who was very strict, didn't see me. I would read several books in a week.

Irene Vaughan

two

Schooldays and Growing up

Temporary education

Until Fairlop temporary school was built children had to attend the Church school at the other end of Mossford Lane – a long walk. Before the main Fairlop school building was completed, some of the older children went by bus to Gearies School for a year.

M. Ellis

Good attendance certificate for Alice Faulkner (S. Dorling's mother) presented by Barkingside school, 1916.

Ivanhoe

In the shadow of Pancake Hill a notable tournament took place. Fired up by reading *Ivanhoe*, a group of us assembled with bikes for chargers, dustbin lids for shields and improvised armour (mine was thick plastic wrapped several times around my corpulent frame). I remember a wild charge at the culminating point of which both my opponent and I missed our targets so we hurtled past each other yelling insults and losing control of our bikes to land in bruised heaps about thirty yards apart. I was even less brave after that and the jousting came to an end, when someone's spokes got bent. The cuts and bruises were impressive and caused comment and, so Mum told me years later, some investigation at school. Mum showed a proper unconcern as 'nothing was broken', but got Dad to inspect my bike. He was concerned about the safety of such activities and bent my ear to no avail.

Roger O'Brien

Fairlop at the Beehive

When I was in the third year of the juniors there was another influx of children from other schools, so they had an annex to Fairlop. It was in Beehive Lane, not far from the pub. They were like wooden buildings and we were bussed there every day. We had our own playground and about four classes.

Linda Reside

Mossford Green church school, *c.* 1920.

Miss Black's Fairlop overflow class
(Beehive Lane), 1952.

Cobbled street

I went to Newbury Park school when we lived in Crown Road. It was always interesting walking to school. Horns Road was cobbled and horses used to slip and slide pulling the coal cart up the hill to Barkingside, especially in winter. Sometimes the tram would help push the car up the hill with the horse pulling with a board in between.

John Knight

Roaming free

I grew up in the Railway Cottages, Carlton Drive, Barkingside. I had a great time as a child. We had trains running at the bottom of our garden, wasteland to the front of the house with a stream running through it, and allotments (including my fathers) to the side. My friends and I virtually ran wild as children, rope swings across the stream from the big elm trees that grew there; fishing for frogs; playing war games, the trains were enemy tanks, and raiding Dad's allotment for peas and gooseberries.

Carol Baldwin

Roding Lane Infants

My first school was Roding Lane Infants and then the Juniors. My first teacher, I think, was Miss Lamas. I had to stay for school dinners and I can still smell that cabbage and see those lumpy potatoes.

Joyce Piggott

Barkingside station hasn't changed, even from Dr Barnardo's time.

Charles Faulkner at Mossford forge.

The Blacksmith's

I remember riders going through the High Street to the Blacksmith down Mossford Green. The rag-and-bone men would keep their horses where the swimming pool is now. It was once a field. From childhood I was horse mad. I would look out for them on my bus home from school and if there were any there, would get off the bus just to go and gaze at them in wonder and admiration. They never took much notice of me. I would then have to walk the rest of the way home but it was worth it.

Faye Pedder

Prefab estate

The prefab estate survived for twenty years only. I was sixteen when we moved out, so during my formative years I lived in a small close-knit community, where everybody knew everybody else and the streets were as safe as our own back gardens. We were surrounded by fields, so there was always somewhere for a growing boy to play, along with a river for adventurous boys to fall in, but it wasn't very deep.

J. Imhof

Earmuffs

I enjoyed my life at Fairlop school and can remember most of my teachers. Mrs

Fairlop School nativity play, *c*. 1953.

Fairlop School, Class 9, *c*. 1953.

Westwood, Mrs Saunders, Miss Tester and Mrs Osborne who wore her hair plaited to look like earmuffs. My two favourite teachers in junior school were Mr Flood and Mr Penny.

Sandra Corderoy (*née* Taylor)

Aunt Lizzie

The last stop whilst shopping was at Frank Norman's, where my Aunt Lizzie worked. My aunt would be standing behind a long counter and behind her were shelves stacked with tin goods, jams, soups in packets and flour. In tubs, oatmeal, tea and sugar were weighed out and put into thick blue-coloured bags. Biscuits were in large tins and mother would buy a mixed selection, sometimes we were given a broken biscuit – probably to keep us quiet.

Patricia Lange (*née* Dawson)

Good and bad

My sisters and I attended Mossford Green County Primary school and then Ilford County High school. I disliked school. My infant years were spent in the Dr Barnardo building. My memories are of being cold, horrible outdoor toilets and warm milk (I still dislike milk). I think added factors were that it was probably less easy to adapt to school then as there was no playschool lead-in, as my own children had. Also, I had assumed I was going to Fairlop

Mossford Primary School, Fairlop Road.

school but the catchment area must have changed when I was taken to enrol. However, by the time of my junior years a new school had been built in Fairlop Road and I was very happy. I had two excellent teachers in Miss Barnett and Mr Newton who instilled the basic three Rs as well as discipline. We sat in rows, received stars for learning tables and a slipper was used by Mr Newton to keep order. My mother is still in touch with people I was friendly with then and I am still friends with Pamela Young (née Stafford) with whom I also went to Brownies and Sunday school.

E. Wood

Three classrooms

I went to school next to Holy Trinity church in Mossford Lane. There were three classrooms in the front of the building and the headmaster's office was at the back. Each classroom had a coal stove for heating and the old-fashioned toilets were round the back.

John Knight

Milk misery

Starting Fairlop school at the age of five I can remember vividly the mixed aroma of disinfectant and creamy milk which I hated. My first teachers were Mrs Hopkins and Mrs Jewell, who seemed very elderly to me. I remember hiding behind polystyrene bricks in the class so as to avoid 'milk time'. I also recall assemblies where we had to sit in rows on the floor in the large hall singing hymns, which I enjoyed. The school hasn't changed much since the 1970s and on returning to vote the smell, that tingled in my nostrils on that first day, still hangs in the air.

H. Kemble

Mud pies

I suppose my first memories were of sitting at the dining room table with Malcolm my brother sitting in the highchair beside me. Sometimes I would help feed him by spooning him his food. As we got older, we used to play together in the garden with a bucket and spade making mud pies. We often slept in the Anderson shelter in the garden. I also remember looking out of the bedroom window at the searchlights criss-crossing the sky and sometimes seeing the flashes of the ack-ack.

V.E. Bush

Scientific panic

My favourite teacher at Fairlop was Miss Wiseman. I still do things she taught us. We had one day a week doing laundry then cookery. It must have been difficult for Mum to supply the ingredients at times with the rationing. We were having a science lesson one day and a bomb dropped on what we called the Prairie. The windows were blown in and the Bunsen burners were alight. There was a panic, then the gas was turned off quickly and we dived under the benches.

Joan Knight (*née* Wright)

Raymond Baxter

I first attended Ilford County High when it was in Ilford. I remember an old notice board there. It referred to the school as 'Park Higher Grade School', from which the name 'Old Parkonians' was derived. A year after I left the war started. This had an enormous effect on the lives of all of us. Only one of my contemporaries who was in my form and survived the war, becoming quite well known, was Raymond Baxter.

Ron Ketteridge

Fairlop Infants and Juniors, built *c*. 1930.

Ilford County High, Freemantle Road. They recently celebrated their centenary.

Queen's ransom

I remember my husband telling me about his time in King George Hospital, Newbury Park. When 'he was about seven years old he had to spend quite a bit of time there. On this particular occasion King George V and Queen Mary were officially opening it. Apparently every child had been given a flag to put over their bed. Just before the King and Queen arrived another child took his flag. My husband's legs were bandaged so he was unable to get out of bed and retrieve it. When the Queen walked past and saw how upset he was she gave him a coin. Unfortunately he couldn't remember what happened to it.

E. Kemble

Moveable school

In 1949 I went to Fairlop Junior school. The Headmistress was Miss Wynne. The following year our year was moved down to Barkingside Village school in Mossford due to lack of space. The teacher there was Mr Chaffer. In 1951 we moved back to the main building and my teacher was Mr Penny. Other teachers I can remember were Mr Paton, Mr Flood, Mrs Osborne and Miss Enoch. She took us for P.E. The caretaker was Mr Grey and he lived in a house on the premises, by Colvin Gardens entrance. We were all scared of him as he looked so fierce. He would tell us off, especially the boys, for climbing on the fences.

Alison Bush (*née* Dryborough)

House captain

I was house captain and played football and cricket for the school. We once played football on Ilford's ground at Ley Street. It must have been a cup match but I cannot remember if we won. The goalkeeper for our team, Norman Agar, went on to play for England

boys and this was announced at morning assembly – quite an honour for the school.

Ray Burton

Dr Barnardo's school

When I came home from Ipswich at the end of 1939 I was sent to Dr Barnardo's school. The Barnardo children had been evacuated and the cottages housed Gibraltarians fleeing their country. I came home at dinnertime until the dogfights overhead made it too dangerous to be out. School dinners were then introduced, brought in by van everyday. We had to go into the brick air-raid shelters and sing loudly during raids. One night the school was bombed, the roof was badly damaged. The

Fairlop Infants, Class 1, 1949.

Fairlop girls' production of *Barratt's of Wimpole Street, c.* 1957.

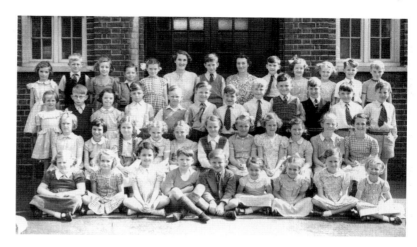

Gearies Infants' School,
1954.

Gearies Infants' School,
1951.

teachers organised lessons in our houses taking six children with a teacher until the school roof was made waterproof. We then went back to our proper lessons.

Joan Knight (*née* Wright)

Donkey

My school-day memories are quite vague but I do remember playtimes when we played five stones, jacks, skipping games and Donkey. The latter was played with a ball being thrown against a wall and when it bounced back you had to jump over it and let the person behind catch it. Each time you failed you added another letter to the word 'donkey' and once you had spelled out the whole word you were out. The teachers I remember are Miss Poynton, my first teacher in Gearies Infants in 1951, then Miss Reis in junior school. She was also involved in the Girl Guides – being a Guide Captain and then local Guide Commissioner. Then there was a male teacher whose name escapes me although I can remember his face – he rapped me over the knuckles with a ruler for talking while

Chigwell school, Chigwell Row 2004.

waiting in line for him to mark our books. It certainly had a deep effect on me as I can still remember it to this day.

Hazel Pudney

Chigwell Row school
When I was five years old I started at the little school by the Green just up past Chigwell Row. I would walk through the forest to get to the school. As we came out of the forest across the road was the Retreat pub, then into the little lane that meets the main part of Chigwell Road. My aunt was taking me to school one day and I had a glider which went right up into the tree. I had to get the Forest Keeper to get it down.

Charles Ernest Winter

Barkingside? A million miles away…
When I was a girl, Barkingside could have been a million miles away. There was no bus service between Woodford Bridge and Barkingside, no 275 then. The only way was to walk to Tomswood Hill. So for people living in Woodford Bridge, Wanstead, Leytonstone and Stratford were our haunts, being on the No.10 bus route. Barkingside and Ilford were difficult to get to without a car, especially for me, as in later years I had moved to Roding

Lane North. It was a long walk down Roding Lane to Woodford Avenue to catch a bus to Ilford, especially in the rain.

Joyce Piggott

Newbury Park Infants
In September 1945 I started Newbury Park Infants' school in Perryman's Farm Road. My mother used to take me with my brother Malcolm walking alongside. My first teacher was Miss York who I seem to recall was quite nice. I remember Miss Williams and the headmaster, Mr Clark. He had silvery-grey hair and wore a black suit.

V.E. Bush

Cycling fun
In senior school you could cycle to school but had to have permission from the teachers and your parents. I remember one teacher called Mrs Malin. She rode this drop-handled racing bike and on one particular occasion she asked me if I was staying to play rounders. I said I couldn't as my bicycle wasn't working. She then suggested I borrow hers, which I had great fun trying to ride.

Linda Reside

Trapped finger
I started school in January 1939 at Mossford Lane next to Trinity church. My teacher's name was Miss Brett. She was so pretty and kind, until I trapped my finger in the toilet door and she made me put it in a cup of warm water and that hurt.

Joan Knight (*née* Wright)

Best seat on the coach
In my school days at William Torbitt, in the mid-fifties, we would be coached once per

Trinity Hall plaque (where Mossford school once stood).

week to Ilford swimming baths. The journey took us down Aldborough Road South where the coach turned right at the end. It became common knowledge that in the upper storey of the corner house stood a bust of a nude. In those days of course, unless young boys were fortunate enough to find a copy of *Health and Efficiency* or *Spic and Span*, (two publications claiming to be naturist magazines), anything showing nudity was hard to come by. For this reason, some of the boys, and remember we were less than eleven years old, would contrive to get a seat on the right-hand side of the bus to ensure a good view. I remember these episodes particularly well because I contrived to sit near to my childhood sweetheart and to let her know that I was above such things in order to impress her. I don't think this had the slightest effect but it didn't go unnoticed by the teacher who complimented me and was glad to see that I was more adult than the other lads. That wasn't the case, but if he wanted to think that, so be it!

Nearly fifty years on, I noticed that the bust was still there. I wrote to the occupier of the house and she kindly replied with the full history of the statue. Apparently, the lady's father attended an art school in 1919 and purchased this 'poor lady without arms' as it became known, carried it home, not very well wrapped in brown paper, on the tram. He was so embarrassed that other passengers gave disapproving looks that he got off well before his stop and walked the rest of the way home.

Geoffrey Gillon

Steaming in

I remember we didn't have much play equipment in the school, then a big steam-roller rolled into the playground. The working parts were taken out and the rollers at the front had concrete round them but we could play on it.

Linda Reside

Open-air school

My first school was Fairlop but I had appendicitis and had to go into King George hospital. Eventually I came out and was told that I mustn't go to school until I was told. I stayed with my gran while my parents were out at work. One day Teddy Dodkins and I were on our way to Valentines Park going tiddling and I had him on the crossbar when the big ginger-haired school board man spotted us and stopped me. They then wrote to my Mum and said I had to go to school. I was too old for Fairlop Juniors and the Seniors were full up. The only place available was the open-air school in Benton Road. It was a school for children who were weak or had been ill. One of my first jobs in the morning was to help this girl who had bad legs. There was

a classroom and the door was open – open air. My job was to rub the girl's feet to get the circulation going otherwise she couldn't walk. You would have a break in the morning when you had hot milk with sugar in it. You would then have a shower. Then dinner. After dinner we would go into a big hall at the side and say if you were number five, you went to number five where there was a stretcher bed and a blanket. You would get your head down for an hour. There were games after this and a few lessons. That was the daily routine. It was a school that 'brought you on'. I was probably the fittest there.

Len Smith

Domino dots and pastels

I started school at Fairlop which I remember as a long, low building with three classrooms down each side of a corridor. The headmistress was a Miss Savage. Some quite poor children attended this school from the remains of a little rural community, living in some very old cottages on the other side of Tomswood Hill. Some had bare feet or wore big hobnail boots without any socks. The school playground consisted of compacted sandy material – not the best to fall over on. Sometimes we found small pale orange lizards; I've no idea what they could have been. We were taught to read using phonetics, and arithmetic using patterns of dots like dominoes. Easy! We had Enid Blyton and *Just So* stories to read, there was plasticine and drawing with pastels on thick dark paper. Also I learned the easy way to thread a needle.

Joan Medlock

Wool

At school we had to learn to knit. The wool was in skeins, not the neat balls you buy today. Before we could start knitting we had to unravel all the wool. It took ages and the wool was very course. The first thing I knitted was a ball.

Sandra Corderoy (*née* Taylor)

Opposite: Fairlop school, Irish dancing class, *c.* 1953.

Right: Form VI Ilford County High School for Girls, July 1937.

Fairlop Infants, 1945

We used a sand tray to form our letters with our fingers and a slate with chalk. There was no paper, very few books and no pens or pencils. We had thick crayons – almost used to extinction. I hated these; even now the smell nauseates me.

Pat Owers

School concerts and fêtes

At the Fairlop school concerts my sister and I dressed up as Pearly Queens and again as Toffs and did numbers like 'I'm Berlington Bertie' and 'We're a couple of Swells'. At school fêtes I never won much except once winning 'guess the number of sweets'. There were halfpenny chews, mojos, blackjacks and lots of unwrapped sweets like peanuts and jazzies. I also won a few goldfish over the years at Fairlop fêtes.

Amanda Ross

The rules of Ilford County High School for Girls

We had to kneel in the hall with the whole school and a lady came along with a ruler and measured your gymslip – either six or nine inches. They would also measure your collars with a protractor. These had to be 60 degrees. As you came out of the door, you had two buttons on your gloves to show the headmistress they were done up. Your velour hat with a band had to be dead straight. In the summer you wore a panama. I had a scholarship to the school as I hadn't lived in the area for more than two years. We received £6 per year and that was supposed to buy your uniform and keep you going. We were not allowed in the park or allowed to speak to boys. One instance was when I met my brother at the end of the road. I was seen talking to him whilst wearing my school blazer and I had to stand with my back to the whole school. We lived in our blazers. I even wore it walking along the front at the seaside on holiday. It was usually the only coat we had.

Mary Baker (*née* Lawrence)

Brilliant teachers

I started Mossford Green Primary school at five years old. Although our teachers stood no nonsense they were brilliant, I still sometimes see Mr Newton and Miss Bowles and it is a delight to talk to them.

Carol Baldwin

Ilford County High School for Boys

I was one of the first boys to go to the new school. As my Dad worked for the Bank of England we had to contribute towards schooling. The paying children had to take three guineas at the beginning of term and hand it in. About three people paid.

John Baker

Houses

At school they had 'houses'. The pupils received points depending on how they performed and these were added to their 'house's' points. There were four houses, Sherwood which was green, Hainault, yellow, Epping, blue and Windsor, red. I was in Hainault and we were nearly always at the bottom and Epping was always at the top.

Linda Reside

Senior school

We had an influx of 'in with the new and out with the old' teachers. The sensible English lessons which I loved were replaced with hippy teachers with psychedelic ideas. It was all too weird and wonderful to me and I could not get on with it at all. To me English was prose, grammar and poetry but I was no longer able to do this. I complained to no avail and then being rather headstrong rebelled and said I would learn English when they decided to teach it again. I was hauled to the head's office and my parents summoned. I

went from being labelled an enthusiastic pupil to a juvenile delinquent.

Carol Baldwin

Crocodile lines

Moving around Fairlop Juniors was done in crocodile fashion. You lined up, put your hands on the shoulders in front for perfect spacing, dropped hands and certainly never spoke. Being late was punishable by your name being taken by the prefects. Three times in the book and you went to the head. Boys were still caned, but not girls. Desks were large, heavy and iron framed. Two sat together. There were rows of two. In our class there were always forty-plus children. Each desk had white enamel inkwells. I was the ink monitor. Each week I fetched an enamel-spouted jug which I had filled with blue ink and went round the class filling all the inkwells. The smell wasn't very nice. We used 'dip-in' pens. I had more ink over me than on the paper because I was impatient and got fed up only writing a few words before dipping again. My work was rather blobby.

Pat Owers

Opening of Gilbert Colvin Primary school, summer term, 1952

I had started school the previous September at Mossford Primary school, classes took place in the lower floor of the school attached to Barnardo's. The Barnardo's school, sited where the magistrate's court is now, used the first floor and we used the ground floor and never the twain was allowed to meet.

My parents knew that I would be transferring to the new school being built in Dacre Avenue. Eventually, during the Easter holidays, a letter arrived giving details of the new school, its opening date (29 April 1952) and informing my parents that I would have a

Derek Lawrence and his brother Gerald in their school uniform.

place in Mrs Hasler's class. I was to arrive with my mum on that morning in the playground. Enclosed with the letter was a small piece of red card (about the size of a postcard) with the letter 'J' written on it in the middle. This, mysteriously, I was to carry as we arrived on the fateful day. Enquiries of my friend Peter Mayes, who was a school year older than me, found that he too had a piece of card and his had the letter 'H' on a blue piece of card.

The day arrived and parents and children headed from all directions to the new school. What we found closely resembled a building site. There was no playground as such, only a gravel-covered area that was to be the playground's substitute for some months. This was to play havoc in the weeks ahead with a large number of knees! Also, the school was

designed for around 250 pupils, but such was the pressure for places, over 400 of us arrived! Before the school even opened, conversions of cloakroom areas into extra classrooms had taken place and, we found, there was no hall or dining room – just a pair of what were to be internal doors firmly locked to prevent children straying onto the building site at the Strafford Avenue end of the school.

As we all stood milling about in the playground clutching our pieces of coloured card, a door opened and out came a portly lady with a matronly bosom (who was, we found out later, Miss Bailey, the head teacher) carrying a chair and a bell. Without a word she placed the chair on the ground, climbed on it and rang the bell firmly, attracting the attention of all. There was a short pause then through the same door came the teachers each carrying a chair in the same way but with a large piece of coloured card on a piece of string around their necks. They climbed upon their chairs and waited.

In no time at all, it dawned upon both parents and children that our pieces of card matched that of the person who was to be our teacher. There was Mrs Hasler with a red piece of card with a large letter 'J' on it. With increasing certainty, we all gravitated towards the teachers matching colours and/or letters as fast as our little brains would allow, or as fast as our mums worked out what was going on. This simple process ensured that each child was in the correct class with the correct teacher in less than ten minutes. No mean feat for over 400 children.

I have been in education for nearly forty years now. I always reckoned that if ever I had the opportunity to open a new school, even now, I would do it the same way. In fact, as a senior governor of a Redbridge primary school, I was thrilled to learn that our deputy head had gained the headship of a new school. We had a conversation about how on earth he was to get all his children in on the first day and I recounted this story. He too was suitably impressed with Miss Bailey's opening gambit and she would be proud to know that it will be repeated.

Derek Lawrence

three

All in a Day's Work

Telephone exchange

When I was four my mother was widowed. I had two brothers and a sister older than me. My mother had to return to work and used to go to the big manual telephone exchange at the top of Fencepiece Road in Manor Road. The building has been converted into posh flats but it was a most imposing telephone exchange. I had seen my mother working there and I thought she looked most impressive; big headphones on her ears and dealing with a cat's cradle of long wires most efficiently.

Faye Pedder

Mallet's

When I first left school I worked at Mallet's. It was in the alley behind Pither's the bakers. We made surgical instruments.

Bert Reed

Claybury hospital farm workers

There were lots of trees (mainly elms) in Claybury Hospital, on the verge of the fence and during the windy times it was not uncommon for them to fall across the road. Men would then come and cut them to clear the road. By

Claybury Hospital, c. 1900.

Victoria House, Cranbrook Road.

Claybury Farm gate there was a gas lamp, which used to flicker eerily. The nurses and people who worked on the farm entered the hospital here and most of them went by bicycle. Their shifts were regular and were twice a day, so at times there were many employees passing by.

M. Ellis

Under-the-counter books

Barkingside Library used to be in the High Street and I would go there on a Saturday and finish the three books we were allowed over the weekend. Later on, I had a Saturday job at Barkingside Library when it had moved nearer the Rec. It was during the years of *Lady Chatterley's Lover* and *The Perfumed Garden*. Such books were kept under the counter and if people asked for them we had to say 'certainly sir/madam but it might not be up to your normal standard of reading'! Naturally we library assistants took the opportunity to read them. It was on a Saturday when I had been working at the library that England won the World Cup. Other Saturday/holiday jobs I had were at Marment's toyshop in the High Street and Sainsbury's where I had to weigh out biscuits and pat up the butter.

E. Wood

National Fire Service

When I was fourteen I left the Scouts and went into the National Fire Service as a messenger based at Victoria House, Barkingside. We were on the top floor with the London Salvage Corp below. It belonged to Barnardo's but this part had been requisitioned by the council. We lived in a house at the end by Tanners Lane. One of our jobs was in Barkingside Park down where the round ring of roses is now. That was an emergency water supply in the war and it was our job to put the standpipe there and run the hoses across the road into Victoria House.

Charles Ernest Winter

Barnardo's, Barkingside

I was living in Brentwood with my parents and I came to Barkingside when I was sixteen years old to work at the Village Home, training for my nursery nursing qualifications. It was the first time I had left home and it was very daunting. My mother left me at Barkingside Station and I had to find my way from there. It was very difficult to find your way about the Village when you first arrived as it was all self-contained. There was a school and a hospital there too. You didn't get a choice of what you had to eat. It was delivered from

Barnardo girls at the Village home. (Courtesy of Barnardo's)

the stores and when they had tripe the whole village smelt of it. Trying to get the children to eat it was bad enough. We used to disguise it in all sorts of ways but they knew. Needless to say, the staff never ate it. I worked at Barnardo's from 1952 to 1955.

Kathy Alston

Paper Round

Before school I did a paper round for pocket money; 10 shillings or 50 pence as it is now. Getting up at 6.30 a.m. seven days a week and delivering the *Recorder* on Thursdays after school. It was a favourite punishment of teachers to give you detention on Thursdays, knowing you had to get the *Recorder* out.

Ray Burton

Fastest milk cart

We used to have our milk delivered by Charlie Duncombe who worked for United Dairies;

first by horse-drawn cart and then by electric milk float.

Alison Bush (*née* Dryborough)

Coal lady

My first job on arriving in Barkingside in 1955 was as a cleaner at Kelvin Hughes. The hours were from 6 a.m. to 8.30 a.m. five days a week. It was very hard work. I worked there for about two years. It enabled me to get home in time to take the children to school. I then worked again as a cleaner but this time in a private house for a lady up in Tomswood Hill. These hours also fitted in with the children's schooling. Enabling me to take them and pick them up as they both attended Fairlop school, which was nice and local. Once the children were older I went to work for a company called Lebons. My job description was Coal Representative. The coal office was in Ilford and the two coal merchants were in Ilford (next door to the

Alison Bush, 2005.

Rose Dean, 2005.

station) and also in Loughton. I covered a very wide area as far as Dagenham, Romford, Hornchurch and Manor Park as well as more locally, in Ilford, Barkingside and Newbury Park. I would travel to and from these areas by public transport or walking and in the latter part of my employment I would use a car. Although I subsequently worked for different companies, I still did the same sort of job. The working day started early. My job included taking orders for coal, as most people had coal-fired heating. You would always see smoke rising from the chimneys. I would also collect the money weekly from the various areas, bank the money and get back to the office to put in the orders for the following day. The job wound up when I was seventy-two years of age. As many changes had started to take place, many had changed their forms of heating and the round had decreased substantially. It was a job I enjoyed for sixteen years.

Rose Dean

Book-keeping romance

I left school in 1948 and started work at United Dairies in Fencepiece Road. I learnt book-keeping and enjoyed earning some money, £1 17s 6d a week; 10 shillings for me and the rest to Mum. There was a good social club at the depot run by one of the milkmen, John. He asked me out and that blossomed into romance and we got married five years later.

Joan Knight (*née* Wright)

GPO

My father didn't serve in the war. He worked for the GPO as a lineman so he was in a reserved occupation. Sometimes at night he took his turn at fire watching, as did most men.

V.E. Bush

Oakside

I worked for over thirty years at Oakside Day Centre for the Elderly at Fullwell Cross. I would do their hair twice a week. They have now knocked this down and it is going to be flats.

Ann Reed (née Croft)

Bus driver

We lived in Crown Road for four years then we moved to Perth Road at the back of the tram depot. My father was a tram driver then a trolleybus driver for forty years without an accident. We didn't stay too long there and moved to Colvin Gardens in Barkingside in 1930.

John Knight

Dad's Army

My father was not in the forces as he was in a reserved occupation, although he had been a regular soldier for fourteen years. He worked for 'Solvent Products Limited' which produced aviation fuel. He was also a member of the Home Guard. His sergeant was Mr Simmonds from the sweet shop opposite the Maypole pub in Fencepiece Road.

Alison Bush (née Dryborough)

Changing jobs

Mr Odell gave me a good school report and reference and I started work at the greengrocers as a delivery boy. I stayed there several months earning 10 shillings a week full-time. I was offered a job by Mr Gibbons the baker, delivering for him from the Redbridge Lane bakery around that area for 12 shillings 6d a week. It was hard work pulling the barrow. One of my customers owned a printing firm and offered me a job there. Being at work earning a little money enabled me to buy a bicycle from a neighbour for £1 10s. Us boys cycled for miles, once to see my relations in Surrey. We would lean

Mr Knight Senior at Ley Street bus depot.

our bikes against the fence at Dr Barnardo's to talk to the girls, but we were soon sent packing. I was at the printers for a year and hoped to get an apprenticeship at Odham's Press in London but I missed the batch of apprenticeships and would have been too old for the next one in four years time, so I left that job and went to work for Sainsbury's in Barkingside High Street. I wouldn't wear Brylcream in my hair so Mr Becker said I could deliver the goods on bike with a basket on the front – mostly to Manor Road and the Bald Hind Hill. Sometimes I would follow the chauffeur who had delivered the order up the hill in his big car. I would deliver the goods to the customer and sometimes she would say, 'Oh, I have forgotten so and so' and I would have to go back and get it. I did that job for a few months and decided to slick my hair down and started helping in the back of the shop skinning rabbits and plucking poultry. When I was seventeen I was sent to Blackfriar's in London on a grocery course. I cycled everyday for two weeks. It was very interesting.

John Knight

Enjoyable chores

Most children had chores to do each day to help their mother or father. I remember sweeping the pavement in front of my mother's shop at 8 a.m. sharp every morning before I went to school. All the other shopkeepers were outside doing the same thing and it became quite a jolly occasion with everybody wishing each other good morning and teasing about missed areas of the pavement. I still sweep the front patio of my house and the pavement but I'm the only person in our road to do so. Old habits die hard.

V. Payne

Making money

When a horse passed your house and did its 'business' you collected it in your bucket and sold it at 1 shilling a bucket. It was a real treat for the roses. Another way to get a few coppers would be helping the milkman with his horse and cart and the bread man with his horse and van.

Brian Taylor

Bicycle cleaning

At school one of the teachers I remember was Mrs Spinks. She had a bike and I would clean it for her and she would probably give me a penny or something for doing it.

Roy Wilkinson

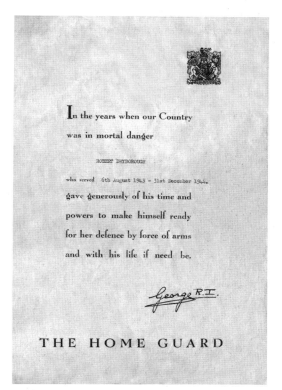

Certificate of Home Guard for Robert Dryborough.

First job at Claybury

When I left school I started my first job in Claybury Hospital as an admin assistant in the Admissions Office. When I was a child we would go to play in the woods in Tomswood Hill, before those enormous houses were built in the fifties, but other children would warn of the 'looney bin' where there were 'mad people'. It used to make me nervous to go there to play. Such ignorance, but I was very young. I could enter the hospital through a door in Tomswood Hill and walk by the tended vegetable plots to the beautiful building. Claybury Hospital was one of the most forward and innovative of mental institutions in Europe in the fifties and sixties. It makes me sad to think that the acres of farmland, where many of the long term patients would work, and woods and fields which provided a haven of peace are now built over. How I wish I had appreciated the eighteenth-century house when I worked there, but I had no interest in the building at sixteen. Claybury Hospital has its own proud history and I worked there for just a year before going for an admin post in the City for BP.

Faye Pedder

The Eagle

The paper round had its perks, as I got to read the *Eagle* comic for free as we delivered comics as well as papers in those days. At least the papers were not so big and heavy, nobody on my round read the *Telegraph*.

Ray Burton

Animal Foods

My mother worked part-time in a pet shop called Animal Foods and after she went full-time, became manageress. She would breed her own budgies and sell them. I remember helping out there and dressing the window when I was about fourteen. It was next door to Redmond's the sweet shop.

Ann Reed (*née* Croft)

A35 delivery service

In the 1950s and '60s, the community was very close knit in Aldborough Hatch and the off-licence seemed to play quite a central role not only supplying alcoholic beverages but also selling soft drinks, tobacco, cigarettes and confectionery. I remember that one man used to regularly buy a whole box of 144 pieces of black liquorice and that others would just come along in the evenings to have a chat. My Father ran a delivery service with his Austin A35 van that was very popular, particularly among some of the older residents who enjoyed their bottles of Guinness or Mackeson Milk Stout. The children always liked the 1d selection of fruit chews, black jack chews and pink shrimps. Also extremely popular were the 1d bags of broken crisps, which I believe were made from the residue in the cooking vats of the ordinary crisps. One of the abiding memories of many old William Torbitt pupils was of these crisps and they were often referred to at a school reunion held a few years ago.

Brenda Graisgour

Fred's Café

My grandparents, Fred and Elizabeth Spicer owned Fred's Café which was situated where the bungalows are now, very near to Greystone Gardens. It was a popular meeting place and the food was known for miles around. It was open all hours and was just opposite the family home in Tomswood Hill. Fred's eldest son, Gordon, worked in the café making suppers, in between his busy family life (a wife and thirteen children).

Jackie Spicer

Aldborough Stores with Mr Graisgour's
A35 delivery van outside, c. 1960.

Fred Spicer's café, 1940s.

LEB husband

After I left school I got a job with the London
Electricity Board as a clerk. This was at their
Head Office in Ley Street, Ilford. I had crossed
the great divide. This was where I met my future
husband, Brian, who already worked there.

Joyce Piggott

Pupil to teacher in seventeen years

Easter 1974 saw me take up a post in Gilbert
Colvin primary school. I was to make the

ultimate transition – leave as a pupil in 1957,
return as a teacher seventeen years later.
Perhaps the strangest part was the reassessment
of the size of the room, grounds etc. I was to
teach in the classroom that I left in '57 and my
memory of a large practical workspace was to
be shattered as I attempted to fit in my class's
tables and chairs. To add to the paradox, as a
pupil I was one of forty-four children working
in that room. I found great difficulty fitting
thirty-two workstations into the same space.
It said a lot about the comparison of teaching

Derek Lawrence, 2005.

styles between Miss Taylor in '57 and me in '74. She had small lift-top desks, neatly set in rows close to one another. Everything from art to maths, music to science, although we only did what she called 'nature study' sitting at our desks. I, on the other hand, was trying to set up a working environment that encouraged movement around the classroom, dedicated areas for art and more display than Miss Taylor would have recognised. Teaching styles had changed. Her full-class lessons to a streamed group of children with one activity, only usually driven from the blackboard, was to be replaced by me organising small groups undertaking multiple activities with a practical 'hands-on' approach.

Derek Lawrence

Fags 'n' Mags

I worked in Fags 'n' Mags (originally Hirst's) near Barkingside roundabout from 1983 to '85 with a lovely local lady called Joan Bond. Her husband Stan had been our school caretaker at Fairlop. The owner of the shop was actually a Mormon priest and lots of American Mormon missionaries used to stay in the flat above the shop. They were so polite and friendly, unlike the owner, who did not display any sign of being a churchgoer. He would have sold his own mother for a packet of Old Holborn.

Amanda Ross

Born and bred

My husband Bob was born in Barkingside at Maypole Cottages, Tomswood Hill in 1922, his

LEB social outing to the races, 1950s.

family having lived in the area for many years. He worked for Lee's doing landscape gardening before I knew him and during our married life he worked for the LEB as a high-tension cable jointer, as did his father before him.

E. Kemble

Apprentice?

I worked at Kelvin Hughes, Barkingside, from about fifteen years old until I was seventeen-and-a-half. I was supposed to be an apprentice learning a trade but we were just like tea boys and runabouts, we used to do sweeping up and cart stuff all round the building and we got bored stiff.

Roy Wilkinson

Tudor Restaurant

I worked evenings in the takeaway fish and chip shop in Manford Way for twelve years so that I could be at home during the day. I worked at one in Ilford before that which had table service as well. I also worked at Gants Hill in the Tudor Restaurant, which was like a café and had tables upstairs and down. It was at the back of Sevenways Parade.

Harriet Dawson

Speed Cop

My Dad was a speed cop, driving a large motorcycle. He was stationed at Ilford 'nick' and patrolled at various times round most of the Ilford, Seven Kings and Newbury Park areas. I remember he was very disappointed when he was assigned to a 'noddy bike' in the late fifties.

John Coborn

Woolworths' staff, Barkingside, 1958.

Ismays

I worked at Ismays at Roding Street, Ilford, as a bulb tester, because my brother worked there. We never had to buy light bulbs. My wages were 3s 4d and halfpenny an hour. I left there after a couple of years and worked for Plessey who were paying more. I went for my interview at Vicarage Lane in 1965. I then had to wait six weeks because they did a lot of Government work and I had to sign the Official Secrets Act and they do lots of checks into your background for anything untoward. I then worked for them at Uppark Drive in Newbury Park, meeting my husband there.

Linda Reside

George E. Gray

George E. Gray the builder/timber merchants were at Katherine Road, Forest Gate when I heard they would be building a place on the corner of Horns Road and Ley Street. I was about nineteen when I wrote to them as I understood they were building new offices and I was desired of obtaining a local job. They replied they were taking their staff with them but would file my name for future reference. Some years later I had a letter to say there was a vacancy if I was still interested. I worked there for four years.

D. Williams

Woolworths

When I was fifteen I got a Saturday job in Woolworths. Before starting we had to take a small maths test. It was very easy as the papers were all re-used and some of the answers hadn't been rubbed out properly. It wasn't like it is now – no self-service. There were different counters and I was on the toiletry counter. I used to love filling up the bath cubes. We sold Rimmel mascara which was in a small flat pot with a brush. We had to wet the brush, sometimes spitting to apply it to your eyelashes. The perfumes I remember were June and Midnight of Paris which was in a dark blue bottle. Everybody wanted to go on the sweet or biscuit counter where a few samples were tried out. The worst counter was electrical because all the light bulbs had to be

The Directors of
W. WAIDE POLLARD & SONS LTD

send you best wishes for a
HAPPY CHRISTMAS

a bonus has been added to your wages
as a recognition of your services
during the past year

Recognition card for
Christmas bonus from
Wade and Pollard.

tested and it was so hot. One day I felt really ill and fainted so I never got to go on there again – thank goodness.

Sandra Corderoy (*née* Taylor)

Various jobs

I was found a job by careers and was placed in a factory in Fowler Road, Hainault. It was for Thorn EMI and I hated it. I was glueing radio faces on and had to drink an issued pint of milk a day to help stop the fumes from the glue coating our lungs. I also worked at Pollard's which I liked but when the manager of Tucker's butchers next door offered me a cashiers job I jumped at it. I didn't realise I would be handling the meat as well. I then got a job in Dewhurst's.

Carol Baldwin

Stonemason

David St Pierre, my uncle was a stonemason. He worked for Ilford Council. David also helped with the gardening at St Peter's, Aldborough Hatch and was rewarded with a letter of thanks.

Peter Cubbidge

Otley Drive doodlebug

In 1943/44 whilst in the National Fire Service, I was on duty with another lad when a doodlebug came over; we heard the bang and the next minute had the message to go. When we got to Otley Drive I had to wade about up to my knees in filthy water as the water main had gone. A fireman was shouting for an ambulance and he had a lady in his arms. I wondered whether she was alive. The blast had taken all the skin off her face; very unnerving for me at fifteen. The end house was completely destroyed, fortunately the man was fine. Luckily his wife was OK as when everything had come down she was in a position that the rafters of the upper floors had held the debris off her. They had only just married.

Charles Ernest Winter

Dinner lady

I enjoyed working as a dinner lady at Fairlop Infants School for about twenty years. There were four of us and approximately 100 children. We had to get all the children in a line. The infants would eat first and then the juniors. It didn't change much during my

David St Pierre (on left) at work, 1970s.

time there but I believe it has changed now. I am sure that most of the children at ages five to seven could read and write because if it was a rainy lunchtime we would have to take the children into the class and either read with them or they wrote. Miss Hope was the headmistress and then Mrs Melnick.

Marjorie Ketteridge

Demob job

I was demobbed in 1946. After a two-week break I went back to Sainsbury's in Cranbrook Road. Our jobs were kept open for us. I didn't like working inside especially watching any army lorries drive by, so my sister Betty, suggested I get a job at United Dairies, Fairlop, where she worked. I started there in August 1948, back working with the older milkmen I had helped as a boy. I was soon given my own round with a horse and cart and served on the new Hainault development at the top of New North Road.

John Knight

four

Leisure and Pastimes

Panda competition

I was one of a team of four that joined the Panda competition competing against other schools. We had to answer questions about the police force. The policeman who was allocated to our school was PC Merry. We were awarded certificates of participation.

Amanda Ross

Football

My school friends and I were very keen on playing football during break times. West Ham was the team that many of us supported. I never went to Upton Park until I was much older. I compensated for this by becoming a supporter of Isthmian Amateur League Club – Ilford FC in Lynn Road. Their ground was a two-minute walk from our house. My match attendance happened to coincide with a rich vein of form that the club were enjoying in the early seventies. I remember being worried that my school friends who went to watch the Hammers might view my Ilford FC support as second rate, but I quickly forgot this as my interest became quite serious. I used to see one of my best friend's Dad who was a home beat policeman at the ground in uniform watching the game. He became a Sunday football team manager for Frenford that I played for briefly. I remember Ilford were finalists in the FA Amateur Cup Final at Wembley in 1974 – the last year the competition was played.

I used to feel a great honour playing for the school football team on Saturday mornings.

Being the goalkeeper, it gave me a feeling of responsibility that I hadn't felt before. Our team manager was the art teacher, Dave Speck, a colourful Norfolk man, who was in his first position as a school teacher. He was our manager for all our five years at the school, giving up his Saturday mornings for the school team. I've seen him since, over twenty-five years later and he hasn't changed at all.

David Goodliff

Barkingside Methodist

Life outside school was very much geared around the church. My husband and I were in the same Sunday school at Barkingside Methodist church when we were three. Twenty-two years later we were married in the same church. I went to Brownies with my friends Elaine and Pam. I would have tea at Elaine's as she lived nearer the church and school and saved my parents a trip. Her mother would inspect us before we left to ensure our badges were polished and shoes were cleaned. My father would collect us and on the way home we frequently bought three pennyworth of chips.

Elizabeth Wood

Lemonade crystals

We had steam trains from Fairlop to Roding Valley for a penny return, and my mum used to give us a bit of bread and cheese or something like that and a bottle of lemonade made out of lemonade powder crystals. We would go off for the day and nobody would worry about you. You could climb over the top of the trains as they were open compartments at the top with a basket to put your luggage. We used to climb into the next truck, climb the length of the train like that and then come back again.

Roy Wilkinson

Conkers

We would walk down Merlin Grove, into Brunswick and then up Penhurst into Tomswood Hill and there was Claybury Farm plus the hospital. We would try and sneak through into the hospital entrance, which was where all the conker trees were. We took our lives in our hands because if you got caught you would have had your ear pulled and frog-marched back to your parents. Policemen in those days could clip your earhole! Kids then respected the law. Obviously most kids had the thrill of doing something you knew you shouldn't be doing and not getting caught. That was all part of the game. We would throw things up to get the conkers down and if there was a brave boy we would send him up the tree and he would get them down although this didn't happen very often. We would pickle them and bake them in the oven to harden them. When we played it was mainly your knuckles that would get hit, and if you hit it too hard the strings that held them knotted together and if you tried to pull them apart it would either go in your eye or bash your knuckles.

Linda Reside

Tripping the light

When I was about five I went to ballet and tap classes at the Hall in Craven Gardens next to the car park. Mrs Norris was the teacher and was very frail. She would sit and play the piano

Barkingside Methodist church, Freemantle Road.

while the class practiced the steps. There were various age groups and I was fascinated how the older girls stood on tiptoe. I remember performing, at the Ilford Town Hall, for elderly members of the community. The dances and songs included 'Bo Peep' and 'Apple for the Teacher'. Our mums made the outfits for us. I still have my baby bronze ballet medal. I also attended Brownies at the Methodist church. After a few years I swapped this for the Gladwys Freestone School of Ballroom and Latin Dancing at Trinity Hall. I obtained all my medals and enjoyed it much more.

H. Kemble

Girls not allowed

When I was ten my father suggested that I attend St Peter Aldborough Hatch, which was nearby. This I did. Although I stuttered very badly I was able to sing very well. I went a few times and then plucked up the courage to ask the choirmaster if I could join the choir. After the service Mr Byng came up to me and said I could join. In 1944 I was singing in the choir and at St Peter we had an enormous amount of weddings. I was able to sing solo at the weddings and received ten bob a time. It was a nice earner for me. One particular time the choir came out on strike because they said that

Mrs Norris' ballet class show at the Town Hall, *c.* 1976.

the other church was getting five shillings and we were only getting two shillings. I didn't strike and was the only one sitting in the choir stalls while the others who still came to the church sat in the congregation. They were on strike for about six weeks until our money went up to five shillings. One day I remember a girl wanting to join the choir. Up to now there had only been men and boys. None of us wanted a girl in the choir so did everything we possibly could to put her off. But she joined and stayed. Yvonne later became my wife. We both still attend St Peter Aldborough Hatch.

Ron Jeffries

Chigwell Homing Society – tribute to Dad

My Dad, James Cove, was a member of the local pigeon flying club. Although he lived in Hainault, they met regularly in the Cocked Hat pub in Woodford Avenue. My Dad organised their social events, the prizes for the races, as well as having all the cups and trophies engraved. He was a member for many years. When he died they held a special evening for him in that pub and presented my mum with a silver tray with all their names engraved on

it. In fact they were affiliated to the National Association and when the members went to the next meeting the week after my Dad died, they held a minute's silence for my dad for his services. I was deeply honoured and know how proud my humble Dad would have been to think that an organisation like that would have a minute's silence for him.

Linda Barnes (*née* Cove)

Lucky escape

I would go to the Ilford Hippodrome every week. One week, we changed our plans and went a day earlier than usual. It was lucky we did. The next night it was bombed. Johnny Mac and an American soldier helped get a lot of the injured out.

Maureen Lewis

Holiday entertainment

In the summer holidays the library would put on events both in-house and in the local parks. I recall one summer day sitting in the Rec with my Mum watching clowns and a Punch and Judy show. Sometimes the library held reading and colouring competitions. I remember having a picture on the wall there and feeling very proud.

H. Kemble

Lantern show

There were several cafés in the area. The Fairlop Café was opposite Johnson's Café and Spicer's Café in Tomswood Hill, which used to be a Saturday night meeting place. We would play the jukebox and drink coffee all night. That would close about midnight. We also went to the State cinema on Saturday mornings where we were ABC minors. I remember seeing Tarzan and Laurel and Hardy; all the old films of the '30s. Before that we started in Mossford Green at the hall near to the church. They used to do a lantern show with no sound, just pictures. Then we transferred to the State as that was the 'in' place to go. When we were bored with that we upgraded and managed to get on the bus to Gants Hill to the Odeon.

Bert Reed

Water fountain in Barkingside Rec.

Happy Valley

My friend Robert and I were both interested in nature and spent hours together looking for birds' nests, catching butterflies, frogs, lizards and the like. We often went to a place known as 'Happy Valley' a couple of miles down Eastern Avenue where there was an abundance of wildlife. I was once bitten by an adder there and had to go to King George Hospital.

John Coborn

Sunday social

As a child I went to Sunday school at the church of St Francis of Assisi, Fencepiece Road. The church was originally the hall and we used to take pennies each week to make a mile of pennies to raise money to build the new church. On a Monday evening we used to pay 3d and watch silent films in the old wooden church hall shown by Mr Day the Sunday school superintendent. This was increased to 6d when he purchased new equipment so that we had talkies. These films included Will Hay, Oliver and Hardy and, of course, the obligatory Hopalong Cassidy, plus cartoons. Once a month, on a Saturday, a social would to be held in the hall with refreshments, which we all attended. In the autumn we had the harvest supper and social.

Alison Bush (*née* Dryborough)

South Ilford Covenanter Leaders, David Dalton and Thomas Anders, 1950.

Saturday morning pictures

Saturday morning pictures were at the ABC cinema at Fairlop roundabout at the bottom of Fullwell Avenue. It was well attended with queues around the block to see the likes of Flash Gordon, Roy Rogers and cartoons. All films were serialised and finished at an exciting part so you came back the following week to see what happened next and if the hero survived. The show always started with the audience of children singing 'We are the minors of the ABC'.

Ray Burton

Soft uniforms

We liked dancing with the Yanks because their uniform was so nice and soft, whereas our lad's uniforms were like khaki blankets. Fights went on, as they weren't particularly liked, especially by the local lads. That is how my husband lost his front tooth.

Irene Vaughan

Backwards and forwards to the matches

I played football for South Ilford Covenanters in 1951 at Fairlop airfield in the Fellowship League. We had no changing rooms. When it rained all our clothes, which we had left on the touchline, were soaked. When the ball went on the runway, sometimes the wind would catch it and then someone had to cycle half a mile to retrieve it. We played once at Newtown Wesley sports ground, which was at Woodville Gardens, at the rear of Barkingside Park. It was like playing at Wembley. They had dressing rooms AND showers! We also played the final at Woodford Football Club as the airfield had then closed. Fortunately this didn't put off our supporters who came by bus to cheer us on. My uncle gave me an old bike to get to the matches. When you turned the cog wheel round the chain would come off because it was buckled so I would have to pedal backwards and forwards. I would do this from Staines Road, Ilford to Fairlop airfield for a game of football.

Brian Taylor

Ramsgill mobile library

Once a week the mobile library came to Ramsgill Drive, nearly opposite St Peter's church, Aldborough Hatch, and this was well used by the adults and children in the area. Not many people had cars in those days, so getting to and from the libraries in the area meant bus journeys, not so easy when carrying heavy books.

Brenda Graisgour

Two-hour outings

We used to take the children from Barnardo's out in big old-fashioned prams with a hole in the middle where they had to put their feet. They sat two each end and we would take them to Valentines Park. We would walk there and back. We would also go to the Recreation Park opposite and often the Matron used to say that we must keep them out for two hours. We would then have to walk round and round the Rec until the two hours were up. On another occasion we took the children over to Fairlop Aerodrome. There was a little bridge over near Barkingside station and we used to go across the fields, which brought you out at the top of the High Street at the aerodrome. We went out one day with two of the three nurses and about three children each and when we got back we couldn't find one of Alfie's shoes. I had taken some photographs and when these came out Alfie was only wearing one shoe at the aerodrome. He had lost it on the way.

Kathy Alston

Canned beans and cocoa

When I turned eleven in the last year of Manford Way School I joined the Girl Guides. I had done a few weeks here and there at the St John's Ambulance Brigade and the Girls Life Brigade, but never stuck it out. So I guess when I joined the Guides my Mother was reluctant when I wanted another uniform. She made me the shirt and bought a navy wool skirt that I could wear even if I stopped going. We met at the Methodist church at the end of Tine Road where I lived. Barbara Pugh was our leader. The dues were tuppence a week

and I was in the Kingfisher patrol. I actually took to it very well and was soon leader of my patrol. I went for badge after badge and soon had an armful. We would go camping at the Girl Guides' camp ground just past Chigwell Row. We would have to scrape punk from silver birch trees and only have to use one match to start the fire. The cans of beans and sausage that we cooked and hot cocoa tasted like the best meal on Earth. We put on shows with the boy scouts and danced with the Essex Folk Dance Society, performing at the church fêtes that they held on the land next to the community centre opposite the Manford Way shops. One Christmas our Girl Guide group went to Dr Barnardo's Home and took out groups of children to parties. As a younger child I had looked over at the houses of the home when passing on the bus and wondered about the children who lived there having no mums or dads to look after them. It wasn't until taking these children out

Kathy Alston, 2005.

with the Guides, did I learn they had house parents who took care of them. I still felt compassion for them but was glad they were not all by themselves.

Patricia Lange (*née* Dawson)

Essex County Cricket

Fred Spicer's youngest son, my uncle Peter, played cricket on the playing field where Fred owned a hut serving food. Peter later went on to play for Essex County Cricket Club and coach over in Sweden.

Jackie Spicer

Winkle Club

During the late 1940s to '50s we joined the Winkle Club with Freddy Inskip and his family from Barkingside. All the members had a little winkle shell painted silver. To get money for the club to go on outings we would have a box that if you didn't have your winkle on you, you would have to put money in it. You might be walking down the High Street or go into a local pub and see a club member. 'Hello Bill, got your winkle with you?', 'Yeah', 'Well get your winkle out and lets have a look'. People would look at you and then when they got their winkle out we explained we were part of the Winkle Club. It was a good atmosphere and other people would join when they saw how much of a laugh we would have. We used to go for outings to High Beech, some would bring salad, some tomatoes and some would bring tea and play games up there. Everyone who was in the club was entitled to come. Sometimes we would go up Hainault one weekend, High Beech another and if you had a car and had room you would put two in with you and the children would have games like the sack race. It would be to keep them occupied more than anything.

Roy Wilkinson

Elizabeth, Fred and Peter Spicer.

Sunday treat

Every Sunday the family would walk along New North Road, past the station where the road narrowed and became a lane with a ditch and hedgerows on either side. I think there were a few shops near to the station entrance. We would walk right to the end of the road, cross over Hog Hill and go into Hainault Forest. This was our Sunday treat.

Jean Westbeech (*née* Thompson)

Tomboy fun

I was very much a tomboy and played with the boys. We had soap boxes or 'jiggers' and would scoot off down the road and it was while playing this that I managed to cut my hand. They would just be a basic long plank of wood, pram wheels off the local dump or wherever, turn it over and where the axel was you laid it across the back end, the big wheels at the back and you put staples round them to keep them onto the wood. The front was the same but narrower and it had a cross piece with nut and bolt under the underside so it would move from side to side. You would have string attached so you could steer it. It was a type of go-kart. You could use your feet to steer as well. A box would be on top so you didn't fall off at the other end and you would have a brake. You would have a piece of shaped wood, angled at one end and that would be nailed to the side of the soap box and when you wanted to stop you would pull it up and it would scrape it along or you could use your hand and that is how I managed to run over my hand. I had a skateboard when I was about seven or eight. It was an ordinary metal wheeled skate with a plank across it which you sat on and went down the hill. If you couldn't turn the corner you just fell off when you got to the end.

Linda Reside

Dick Barton

We loved Dick Barton – Special Agent, on the radio. It kept you gripped. There was also a space serial which was really frightening. We listened to *Grand Hotel* with Max Jaffer and *Over the Garden Wall* with Gert and Daisy. We had a wind-up gramophone and three records – Tchaikovsky, Grieg and George Formby singing *Leaning on a Lamp post*. I played these again and again. We had an ancient piano that only played a few notes. It was wooden framed with candlesticks on the front.

Pat Owers

No Sunday boating

My husband, John, took his birthday boat down to Valentines Park when he was about seven years old, but it sank. The rules for

Sunday in the park were that no games were to be played. I remember going to the open-air swimming pool there. There was also a boat in the park that people went in for a ride if they paid a penny each.

Mary Baker (*née* Lawrence)

Blake Seven fan club

I started a Blake Seven fan club with some school friends after the hit television series. I don't think it lasted very long but we managed to make membership badges and transportation devices out of cardboard.

Amanda Ross

Redbridge sports centre

Norman Booth started the sports centre about thirty-two years ago and it has grown and grown. We joined and became life members. I remember one fundraiser was a sponsored walk to Epping sports centre and back. My daughters and I joined in this. The centre has made a difference to our lives. It has been a real benefit to the community. I still play tennis there and my wife and I are actively involved.

Ron Ketteridge

Grange Farm

The children played over Grange Farm more as there weren't many children over there and they could roll up and down the hill. The children would walk towards the King's Head at Chigwell then cut through the pathways. Jeye's Disinfectant had a big building near there.

Harriet Dawson

Scooting with girls

I didn't have a car when I was younger so I purchased a scooter. I would go to dances

Above: Playing fields at Fairlop (now part of Redbridge sports centre).

Right: Brian Taylor's scooter.

at Manor Hall, Chigwell, dancing to Reg Corvell's band. It was hard taking girls home on the back of a scooter though.

Brian Taylor

Penny for the Guy

All the kids in our little area would club together and build a brilliant Guy, usually using a pair of my dear neighbour, Mr Lambert's, trousers. Mr Lambert was a stout man and it took many newspapers to stuff the bottom of the guy. We would spend weeks scouring the neighbourhood and fields for wood, several of us dragging home huge branches. The gigantic bonfire would be on the wasteland. Guy money and contributions from everyone's parents ensured a bonfire night to remember. We would go with Dad to Lee's Garage in Horns Road and get a can of paraffin to ignite the fire. The night would be transformed by Jumping Jacks, Catherine Wheels and rockets. After the bonfire we would go back to my house for jacket spuds, Tizer and R. Whites lemonade. Wonderful days!

Carol Baldwin

Church life

I was probably one of the first children at Gants Hill Methodist church in Gaysham Avenue when it was built. They built the hall as there were so many people attending but a few years ago they sold it because it wasn't used. My parents would walk after church across the fields towards the Dick Turpin at Aldborough Hatch. I would sit outside and have an arrowroot biscuit. The whole of Sunday was taken up with church or Sunday school services.

John Baker

Flash Gordon

My brothers, sister and I, along with a gang of friends, always went to the State cinema for Saturday morning pictures. We wouldn't have missed it for anything. We would see Flash Gordon and of course Superman – not to mention westerns. We had 1 shilling each (I don't know how my Mum afforded it). It cost 2d each way on the bus and 6d to get in. The other 2d was to spend on sweets at Enever's, which was next door to Grange Hill Station where we got the bus. We probably drove old Mr Enever mad choosing our sweets.

Linda Barnes (*née* Cove)

Gants Hill Methodist church outing, 1930.

Dick Turpin, Aldborough Hatch, 1900.

Mr Baxter's woodwind class at Fairlop Juniors, *c.* 1977.

Blackberrying

When we moved to Forest Road in the fifties army huts were still behind but they were used to house the unhouseable. Beyond that was a wonderful area for picking blackberries. You can even now walk across Fairlop Waters to the rough land and still pick blackberries.

Ron Ketteridge

Woodwind lessons

Whilst at Fairlop Junior school I was lucky enough to learn the clarinet with Mr Baxter. I didn't mind playing tunes but the scales we had to learn were pretty boring.

It did, however, open a few doors for me. It was assumed that by being able to play an instrument and read music, you could also sing. Thus, I auditioned and was chosen to take part in the Redbridge Choral Festival at the Royal Albert Hall and on another occasion some of the school were filmed by the BBC for *Songs of Praise*, from the church at Barnardo's. I gave up clarinet lessons when I was in the second year of seniors as it interfered with my maths lesson. Needless to say, it probably would have been more beneficial to carry on with the music!

H. Kemble

five

Wartime
Experiences

Temporary glass

Our houses backed on to Claybury and one Sunday whilst we were having lunch a bomb dropped into the fields and smashed all our windows at the back. Whilst helping to pick up the glass I managed to get some in my hand and I was carted away to hospital. I had a lift there but had to find my own way home after it had been removed. Brown paper-like cardboard was placed over the windows until they repaired them with a temporary wartime glass, which was imperfect.

Irene Vaughan

Shelters in Aldborough Hatch

During the Blitz we had an Anderson shelter in the back garden and spent every night down there. I can remember the Saturday afternoon when the docks caught fire. There was a massive explosion. We then had a Morrison shelter indoors which we used and my parents also bricked up the bay window at the front of the house, as there were quite a few bombs around here. I remember the children collected shrapnel but quite a bit of what you found wasn't the real thing.

R. Jeffries

My German dachshund

My mother's shop repaired watches, clocks and jewellery. There was a German prisoner of war camp nearby and a prisoner would come in to buy materials to repair the watches of other prisoners in the camp. He was very nice and told my mother that he was very worried about his mother and sister who lived in Hamburg, as there had been so much bombing there. He said he couldn't understand why two countries that had so much in common and such strong ties within our royal family should want to fight each other. He liked the English people very much but missed his country. He made me a toy. It was an articulated dachshund on a platform. As I pulled it along, it swivelled and looked almost real. It was painted white with black spots. I adored it and have always wished I could meet this German soldier to thank him for the pleasure it gave me. He was repatriated after the war and my mother had a letter from him to say that his mother and sister had been killed during the bombing and thanking her for her kindness to him. She never heard from him again.

V. Payne

Pathé News

At the State cinema we sat in the cheap seats – 6d – and I loved the Pathé News, our only way of knowing how the war was progressing

Pat Owers

Italian prisoners

On New North Road, opposite Hainault tube station was an Italian prisoner of war camp and the inmates could be seen wearing donkey jackets with POW written on the back. They used to make wooden toys, which they gave to local children. I also remember spending time in our air-raid shelter because of the doodlebugs. It was a frightening time.

Ray Burton

Bombing out the brave

After a bombing raid the streets were full of rubble. There was always a group of people searching through the remains of their houses, collecting things and putting them into prams, wheelbarrows or carts. They seemed so brave to me. Nobody cried they just got on with collecting their things. Rescue gangs and ARP's were everywhere. They were mostly old men and looked very tired. My mother would say, 'Poor souls, they've been up all night in such and such road, it was bombed last night'.

V. Payne

R101

One of my earliest memories as a child was of the R101 airship and when that came across. Everyone was pointing down from Hainault and I saw it in the sky. It must have been the

same weekend because I remember it again. We had been to St Winifred's church at the Bald Hind and when we came home we got off the bus at the Maypole, Chigwell Row. There was this noise in the sky and I remember seeing the blackness and the lit up cabins. I didn't know what they were then. I recall R101 was being mentioned by some people.

Charles Ernest Winter

Above: Ray Burton in his air-force uniform.

Right: Original Chigwell Row cottages, 2004.

Coal

A recycling scheme Dad had was making coal-dust briquettes with a little cement and water poured into wooden moulds that he made. Nothing was wasted and I am the same today, except for the coal.

Joan Knight (*née* Wright)

Dahlias

A German prisoner of war managed the farm shop at Fowler's Farm (now Forest Farm). He had stayed over here after the war and married a local girl. He didn't have a trace of a German accent. He grew those gorgeous dahlias in the front garden of his cottage in Forest Road.

Ron Ketteridge

Bombs

The gun camp by Fairlop station was over the back of our house and I can remember seeing the searchlights swinging around the sky at night, also barrage balloons were a common sight. Often the planes from Fairlop would take off over our house with a bomb under each wing. There was an ARP hut opposite Johnson's Café with sandbags outside. There

was a V2 rocket dropped behind our house, blowing the back of the house in. All the windows went, the bathroom one ending up on the landing. They came and patched us up until they got round to putting in glass.

Alison Bush (*née* Dryborough)

Yanks

They had extraordinary rations did the Yanks – always chocolate. Two of my friends married American soldiers and went back to the US. The girls had to have a clean record and clean bill of health. They were only sixteen when they married.

Irene Vaughan

Hainault estate

Work started on a building project in 1945. At the time there was an Axis prison camp at the junction of Hainault Road and the Eastern Avenue; these soldiers were used to construct the prefab estate. In many places the names of the prisoners were written in the wet cement, leaving a poignant reminder for a generation to come. On the opposite side of Forest Road was Fairlop airfield made famous

View over Fairlop taken from No. 16 Fencepiece Road.

during the Battle of Britain, its buildings and air-raid shelters were still in place well into the sixties.

John Imhof

Red sky at night

In 1940 every household took delivery of an Anderson shelter to be dug in the back garden. My Dad took the fence down and stood it in front of the dining-room French window and piled the earth up against it. That's where it remained for the rest of the war. The Blitz was a frightening time, air-raid warnings went off during the day and night. Nobody slept properly for over seventy nights – the sky was red with the fires in London.

Joan Knight (née Wright)

Almost losing face

Fairlop aerodrome was a Spitfire station and in the field at the back of our houses in Fencepiece were four big ack-ack guns. When anything came to bomb the aerodrome these guns would go off to hit the planes up in the air. One day I was sitting in the back room with the dog, facing the window and my sister and her boyfriend were facing me. We had an old mattress with no inners which we rolled down over the window to use as blackout. Suddenly we heard a whoosh. The boyfriend told us to get down on the floor. He said that there was a bomb nearby. Down at the bottom of the garden was a crater 15ft deep and 20ft in diameter. If we had had a shelter, we wouldn't have been here as that is usually where the shelters were. We went out there looking for shrapnel, and I fell down the hole. The soil was soft and hot. I was looking for the nose cap of this bomb. I didn't realise but it blows to pieces, so I got back out of the hole with a struggle. The next minute there was an ARP warden, who used to patrol the

street, with his helmet on and a couple more people and we were all standing round the hole. We heard somebody shouting 'HELP, HELP!'. There was this girl coming across the field. The ARP warden asked her what the matter was. She said she had been walking across the field with her boyfriend and he had been hit in the face, blowing all his face away. Two bombs had dropped in the field, one in Fairlop school and two in Claybury grounds, but as luck would happen no one was hurt. It never hit any buildings, only fields or gardens. Anyway, this girl didn't know what to do. So all of a sudden he rolled up and he was covering his face and groaning. The ARP-warden said to come here so he could take a look. Anyway he had a look and said, 'You're alright'. 'What do you mean?' he said, 'my face is killing me and it's all open.' 'No,' the warden said, 'it's a tomato.' It was one of my dad's ripe tomatoes; it must have hit him

Roy Wilkinson in his back garden, late 1940s.

Mr R. Dryborough, a member of the Barkingside Home Guard, outside the State cinema (front row, eighth from the left), 1940s.

in the face. His face was covered with pips and tomato skin. When we told him what it was he was a lot better, but it still hurt him.

Roy Wilkinson

Get out quick!

I remember being woken up one night. I saw cot bars so I must have been very young. I was hurriedly stuffed into a siren suit and carried at great speed downstairs and out into the garden. It was very cold and misty and I remember loud explosions, which didn't frighten me at all, but I remember my mother crying out 'Lord protect us'.

V. Payne

Shelter on the stream

Our Anderson shelter was at the bottom of our garden in Fencepiece Road and was always flooded as after it was dug out and erected

it was discovered there was an underground stream there. We only used it rarely and I can remember my Dad in Wellington boots lifting us over onto a bunk. The only lighting we had down there were candles in a lantern. Us children thought it was fun as we did not realise the danger. If the bombing was not too heavy we slept on the living room floor.

Alison Bush (*née* Dryborough)

Vegetarian rations

My mother registered my sister as a vegetarian as you would get extra rations of vegetables, cheese and nuts. My mother always said to us, 'If you see a long queue, join it!' I remember queuing at 'a shop in Ilford Lane to get horsemeat for the dog, but many people would use it themselves as meat was minimal. We were fortunate because we had the rabbits and extra vegetables from the allotments.

Ron Jeffries

Sheila Dorling outside the Co-op – note the rationing notices in the window displays, 1940s.

Bomb on your doorstep

During the war we lived off Horns Road. We woke up one morning to no doors or windows. A bomb had landed in a field on the other side of the train lines. They were trying to get to the ammo factory. We never even woke up when the bomb exploded. I guess we were used to the noise. One of the most memorable events of the war years was when a German pilot bailed out of his plane and landed on the roof of the tobacconist, just down from the police station. He would not come down until the police arrived, as he was afraid of getting mobbed.

Maureen Lewis

Victor Values

When I was fourteen I got a job with Victor Values in Gants Hill. I had to drive a pushbike with a little wheel on the front delivering all their orders; they were a food and cut-price shop. We served all the Jewish area at Clayhall as they did kosher food. One day they said I had to go up Saturday morning and deliver round East Ham because their driver hadn't come in. So straight away I said, 'Do I get extra?' 'Ooh,' he said, 'you might get a bit extra.' I told him that I wasn't cycling all the way to East Ham and do their work and my work for nothing. Anyhow they sent me up to East Ham and loaded me up with the food. I got to East Ham Town Hall and the siren went. The police said, 'Quick, leave your bike and get in this shop.' They had a big meat freezer at the end and they shoved us all in the meat freezer for safety. I left my bike out the front with the food on it. While we were in there the policeman said that he had stopped us because a bomb had landed in East Ham. It had come down on a parachute and was hanging in the trees. They were frightened it might go off and while we were in there it did. Glass went everywhere. When I came out of there the eggs were broken in the bike, but we were all right. When I went back to the shop, the manager came out and asked where I had been. I told him, but all he wanted to know is whether the goods were all right because it was all rationed. I wasn't happy. Of course, when he came out he saw that the eggs were broken. I told him that he was more worried about the eggs being broken than he was about me. So I packed that lark in – I didn't want that job no more.

Roy Wilkinson

Werner Bähr at Fairlop POW camp, 1940s.

Mickey Mouse and bad news

I remember being issued with a Mickey Mouse gas mask. I wouldn't wear it because it smelt so horrible, looked horrible, and I couldn't breathe. It was bright blue and yellow I think. The only other wartime memory was the huge Sherman tank thundering along Barkingside High Street. It had soldiers on it and people were shouting and cheering. Telegrams were sent for speedy messages. My mother dreaded these in case something bad had happened to my father in the war. A young boy would bring the telegram on a motorbike.

Pat Owers

Escape to Harwich?

In 1944 the doodlebugs (V1) started. They were mainly aimed at London but they flew over Barkingside. Dad decided we would be safer by the coast so we got permission to go to Mum's sister at Harwich. Mum was expecting a baby and we got there with just four days to spare before my sister Marianne was born. Mum had just had the baby when the air-raid warning went off and a doodlebug flew between Harwich and Felixstowe going on to crash at Ipswich. You couldn't escape anywhere. I went to school at Harwich for a while – the whole town was busy with thousands of troops, we wondered why but it turned out to be preparations for D-Day.

Joan Knight (*née* Wright)

Zeppelin

The one thing that stands out in my mind is 13 October 1915. It was the night of the Zeppelin raid and my younger sister was born. The chief things were the airships coming over. I remember an airship coming down in flames at Cuffley and everyone thought it was much nearer as it was just balls of flames.

D. Williams

POWs

Where the sports centre is now was the German POW camp. Clement Attlee suggested that POWs be released for a few hours at a weekend and if any families would be willing to take them in showing them a bit of British hospitality. This we did. One in particular sticks in my mind. Karl-Heinz Rüping. He was seventeen years old and was taken prisoner at Arnham. The other was Werner Bahr. We used to have them at weekends and then escort them back to the camp. On a particularly cold day in 1947 I gave Karl-Heinz an overcoat. He was most grateful. After the war they both returned home.

Charles Ernest Winter

No stopping the tanks

The tank traps would go the length of the railway. They were big two-metre squares of concrete in the ground. There was also iron bent in a 'U' shape in the ground to stop the tanks in an invasion. When you see the tanks they had, they would have just driven over the top.

Roy Wilkinson

Wartime worries

We had quite a happy time during the war. Being so young I wasn't aware of what bombs were or the dangers. We used to go upstairs to the couple in the maisonette above and watch the doodlebugs. I can remember the worry of my mother and relief when the noise stopped and the wind blew the V1s away from us. Then there would be a silence followed by a thud. All through the war the sirens would sound. At first we went to the Anderson shelter that Dad had built in the garden but I was terrified in there. It had about a foot of water in it and the wooden planks were slimy. It smelt musty and so claustrophobic. Soon after we just stayed indoors cowering under our wooden table. The roaring of the planes still lives with me.

Pat Owers

Blown out

My aunt lived in a house in Old Blind Lane off Tomswood Hill. It was a ritual on a Sunday they would have their dinner then go and have a lie down. I was sitting having my dinner with my home-guard uniform on when we heard a doodlebug, which cut out, and that was the finish. All of a sudden there was a bang. I couldn't finish my dinner because the window came in and showered it with glass. I called out for my mother but couldn't find her. She was laying in the back garden. She had been seeing to dinner when the blast had blown her up against the gas stove and whether she got panic or fright but had gone into the garden and passed out. The first thing she said when she came round was 'Sooky', who was my sister, so I went to her cottage up the road to check if she was all right. Laying in the road was the milk lady. From her ankle right the way up it looked like someone had cut it with a knife. I then checked at my aunt's. She had been blown out of the bedroom window and landed on the floor but didn't have a mark on her. Carrying on down the road was a bungalow or two. They had disappeared except for a water tap. There was a man standing there with one ear missing filling a saucepan with water. Being in a panic as I was, I said for him to come with me to

Joan and John Knights' wedding at Holy Trinity, 1953.

the corner of the road where the NAAFI tea wagon had pulled up. He said he had to put the fire out first. He was in shock. There was nothing left of his bungalow. It wasn't until after that I felt as sick as a dog.

Len Smith

Gathering swedes

Coming along Blind Lane, down Hamilton Avenue from the Cranbrook Road (it is now Ashurst Drive), was a narrow bridle path called the Horseshoes. In about 1917 I remember walking up the Horseshoes and on the right-hand side there were prisoners of war gathering swedes. I remember it so well they used to want to be friendly and at the sight of children they would try to communicate with us.

D. Williams

Evacuation

On Friday 1 September all the children and the teachers assembled by the police station, got on the bus to Ilford station then a steam train. My Mum had packed new clothes and bought me some nuts and raisins to eat. She said, 'Don't forget to clean your teeth' and off we went. Us children at five years old thought it was a school trip. We arrived at Ipswich railway station and were taken to a school to sleep for the night. We were given a bun, a banana and a small bottle of milk and shown to a camp bed in the big hall. We had been evacuated. My Dad brought me home in December, for my sixth birthday. I kept in touch with the Park family with whom I had stayed, until 2002.

Joan Knight (*née* Wright)

six

Home Life

Spicer family

The Spicer family of Barkingside strongly believed in the family all working together and they were a well-known family in Barkingside. Fred Spicer was the first one in Tomswood Hill to own a car and television, which was quite an achievement then.

Jackie Spicer

Indoor bathroom

As my father was a builder we were lucky enough to have an indoor bathroom. All our neighbours had an outside toilet. In the winter the freezing cold and darkness made a visit to this necessary establishment a very hurried exercise. Our next-door neighbours would emerge from the back door muffled in warm coat, scarf and carrying a torch. In the summer it was a place to visit for pleasure. A newspaper or a book would be taken in and a long session ensued.

Fred Spicer outside his house in Tomswood Hill.

Going up to bed was achieved in record time. Having had our bath in a freezing bathroom earlier in the evening, we sat cuddled up in thick winceyette nightclothes, slippers and a thick dressing gown. We always had a hot milky drink before going to bed as my mother believed that we should be warm inside and out.

V. Payne

Winter warmer

In the winter to heat the hall space we used an oil heater, which let out a distinctive odour. The bedrooms were not heated at all and I remember getting undressed and into bed as quickly as possible to avoid the cold or undressing in the dining room in front of the fire. Our beds were warmed with hot water bottles. Even though we had three bedrooms, we never used all three as bedrooms, so I shared a room with my sister. I do remember the time when we had central heating installed but when this happened I am not sure. From then on all the rooms in the house would be used on a regular basis.

Hazel Pudney

Street games

We played games in the street. These were either skipping with one end tied to the lamp post; cricket, using a dustbin for a wicket and sometimes marbles. There was no traffic in those days so it was quite safe. Sometimes our

Ray Burton, 2004.

Mrs Croft's house in Craven Gardens.

parents would join in or shout encouragement from garden gates.

Ray Burton

Steadman houses

I lived in a privately built three-bedroomed house. The builder who built them, Mr Steadman, lived next door to us. I was friendly with his daughter. The road, Craven Gardens, wasn't made up, only the top half towards Barkingside station and then it stopped and was old pit holes. This was probably where one builder stopped and another took over. The houses are different if you look now.

Ann Reed (*née* Croft)

Hardcore

There were no such places as recycling places or refuse tips as we know them today. If you had anything you wanted to get rid of there were dumps you could take things to or the rag-and-bone man would take any metal and rags. When my Dad knocked down the old coal bunker there was no way of getting rid of the rubble so he dug a great big hole at the bottom of the garden putting all the rubble in, topsoil over the top and put grass on it. The same happened with the people next door who were building a lean-to. They needed all this hardcore and my brother had an old go-kart so that went in there and bits of engine, old tyres, anything to make up the hardcore.

Linda Reside

Cranbrook Road opposite Victoria House looking towards the Chequers pub, 1930s.

Doctor, dentist and a fish tank

Our doctor was Dr Barry, who ran his surgery from a house in Southwood Gardens. I can remember him as a friendly Irish man. If we needed to see him we just went along in surgery hours and waited our turn in the waiting room.

My first dentist had his surgery in Great Gearies – a big house in Cranbook Road where Barton Meadows is now. I remember it well as the frontage had grand railings and we had to walk up a long path to the front door. I also remember they had a fish tank in the waiting room.

Hazel Pudney

Medicine and money

Each day my sister and I were dosed with a spoonful of halibut oil and malt, also cod liver oil but I could never keep mine down. We wore liberty bodices to keep warm in winter and often had our chests coated with Vick. Iodine was dabbed straight onto cuts and grazes. Mum had 17s 6d a week to live on from the army. Our rent was 12 shillings 6d so there was very little money left. At about eighteen months old I had ronchial-pneumonia and nearly died. This cost 7 shillings 6d for the doctor to visit. Thankfully I did survive. To implement income Mum cleaned a few houses in Tomswood Hill.

Pat Owers

Beauty spots

At the bottom of my road on New North Road crossroads stood the Maypole pub. On a Sunday morning a man used to set up a shellfish stall in front of the pub and it was my job to get shrimps for my parents and winkles for my brothers and I for Sunday tea. We would remove the winkles and thread them onto a string until we had emptied all the shells, before eating them with bread and butter. The black caps we would stick on our faces to the consternations of our parents. If other relations were coming to tea on a Sunday we would have a jelly and they would always bring an offering, cake or sandwiches to help out.

Ray Burton

Chimney sweep

The chimney sweep was fun. On his annual visit he would arrive with his array of rods and brushes. Newspapers and sheets would adorn the front room. He would come in, look up the chimney to assess the angle then set about joining all the rods together. He would then heave, twist and push, and us kids would run into the garden to await the appearance of the brush at the end of its journey out of the top of the chimney. Occasionally a poor dead bird, which had the misfortune to fall down the chimney and become trapped, would be found all black and mummified from the smoke.

Carol Baldwin

Doctor's orders

I remember going with my father up the road on a Friday evening to Mr Burrell's house to pay his subscription to HSA for the doctor and hospital before the National Health came in. Our doctor was Dr Findlay at No. 2 Fencepiece Road. At the right-hand side there was a window, which was the dispensary. That was done away with when the National Health Service came in and you got your prescriptions from the chemist, which was Parrott's. Eva Hall worked in there.

Alison Bush (*née* Dryborough)

Traditional meals

We lived in a council flat on Duke Road and a council house on Princes Road, eventually buying the house from the council. Bath nights were on Friday, laundry was done on Monday. We ate the usual English meals – bangers, fish and chips, beans on toast, shepherd's pie and on Sunday we would have roast beef with Yorkshire pudding.

Maureen Lewis

Fluffy white towels

Monday was washing day and my Mum had an old copper that she used. Before we had

the emersion heater to heat the water we had two coal fires, one in the front and one in the back. The back one was used on bath night, which was normally a Saturday or Sunday. The fire would be stoked up with coke and that would heat the water in the back boiler. When we were little we had a tin bath in front of the fire and Mum would hang all the white towels on the rail protecting us from the fire and both my sister and I would bathe together. Then Mum would put this lovely big warm fluffy white towel round you. It was wonderful.

Linda Reside

Move to Barkingside

We moved to Fencepiece Road, Barkingside, in October 1955 from Leytonstone. My husband was working at the Hainault Industrial Estate for Fletcher Brock & Collis as an

Mr and Mrs Dryborough's wedding photograph outside their house in Fencepiece Road, c. 1930.

engineer at the time, so it was a good idea to move nearer to his place of work. Up to now he would cycle from Leytonstone to Hainault every day. We were also renting in Leytonstone and wanted a bigger place of our own for the family. The move from a built-up area to Barkingside seemed like a move to the country. The fields behind our house (which are now playing fields) were very barren. Many used the field as a cut-through to Fairlop station and Forest Road.

Rose Dean

How things change

I had two younger sisters who shared a bedroom, whilst I had the box room, apart from a short period when my grandmother lived with us. Domestic life was very different from now and far more arduous. The washing was boiled and then mangled; the sheets were folded by standing at each end of the hall. My father had detachable shirt collars that went away in a box to be laundered each week. We did not have a television until I was seven and for special occasions such as the Coronation we went next door or to my friend Elaine who lived in Waterloo Road who had a television before us. There was no central heating so each day fires had to be laid and the boiler raked out. It was cold going upstairs to bed and I disliked the moment of leaving the room with the coal fire. I also hated the odd occasions when I had to come home to a cold house and light the fire. We did not always have a telephone but we must have had one when I was eleven since we had a day off school on the day of Princess Margaret's wedding. This was also eleven plus results day so there were frequent phone calls to see who had passed. Cooking was geared more to days of the week, with roast on Sunday; mince (done in a mincer) on Monday and was generally the traditional meat and two veg. Puddings were frequently served with custard and food such as fruit, cream and peas, often tinned. When I visited my grandmother we would have ham off the bone and cakes with real cream as a treat. We did not at first have a fridge and food would be kept at the neighbours.

E. Wood

Saturday evening paper

Every Saturday evening I would go with either my Mum or Dad down to Hirst's at the end of Tomswood Hill to await the *Evening Standard* paper. There would be so many people packed into the small shop. When the papers arrived it would be a bit of a scramble as nobody had managed to queue, then home to check the pools results. During the day my Dad would let me go down to Hirst's on my own to get him his ½oz of Old Holborn or Golden Virginia and a packet of greens. There was never any question of who it was for as the owners knew their customers well. Dad sometimes had tobacco in tins and when he had used the tobacco they became good storage containers for holding bits and bobs in the garage.

H. Kemble

Worst winter

The worst winter was in 1947. When my sister married on 31 March of that year there was still twelve inches of snow on the ground and there was nowhere to put it. It didn't melt. We took hot water bottles in the car to the church. My father had a greengrocery round and couldn't get to the wedding on a Saturday so my sister married at St Laurence, Barkingside, on a Sunday. Holy Trinity didn't marry on Sundays.

Irene Vaughan

Right: Holy Trinity church, 1930s.

Below: Brian Taylor, 2005.

Recycling

We couldn't afford much furniture for the bedroom so I made a cabinet to keep my clothes in from an orange box turned on its side. A shelf would be in the centre and my mother made a curtain for the front. It certainly did the job. My brother and I shared a box room in our house, and also clothes. When my brother grew out of something I knew that it would then be mine.

Brian Taylor

Bath-time sounds

Washing day was mostly Mondays as the washing had piled up after the weekend. Washing was done with a rubbing board and a tin bath. We had a mangle in the garden to squeeze the water out. The council gave you a boiler to boil it in and it went by gas. It was more luxurious than the one in the house before as we had to light a fire to get hot water. To get your water upstairs for a bath you had a handle which pumped it. Everyone knew when next door was having a bath because we could hear the noise of the pump.

Harriet Dawson

Rabbits

We had rabbits in our back garden and it was my job to look after them. I would ask over the allotments for carrot tops and various other greenery cut from the vegetables, put them in a little cart that I had and wheel them home for the rabbits. My father would fatten up a rabbit and every other Friday he would use the iron stick that my mother used for poking the washing in the copper to bring about its end. We never ventured outside when this was going on!

Ron Jeffries

Yes, Matron

I had to go into King George hospital on one occasion and I thought it was very clean. As you lay in the iron bed they would dust around you. The bed covers had to be straight. Matron ruled the roost. The nurses were smart and their uniforms were beautiful. When I had my daughter, nurses from Paddington hospital were working in the Ilford Maternity hospital. I think St Mary's had been hit during the war and they had been transferred.

Mary Baker (*née* Lawrence)

Indoor cricket

In 1950 we had to make our own amusement so we would play indoor cricket. My brother made a small cricket bat out of wood, which I still have. It was three-and-a-quarter feet long. You would also need two empty brass shell cases approximately six feet high for wickets (my father brought these home from the Woolwich Arsenal) and a marble. Eleven soldiers would be placed round the room as fields. We would then bowl the marble. If it hit the shell it makes a 'ding' noise and you were then bowled out. Hit a soldier [toy] then you were caught out. If the marble hit a wall with a bounce then you scored six. Hit the wall along the ground then score four. Fortunately, we had our mum's permission to play in the front room. This would keep us amused for ages.

Brian Taylor

Inside a prefab

Each prefab was detached; had two large bedrooms to the right of the front door, a toilet and separate bathroom to the left; in front of a short passage was the lounge with a kitchen to the extreme left. The kitchen was fully fitted with an electric cooker, an electrically heated copper for washing clothes and a fridge. Next to the larder was a pull-down table for meals. The front of all the prefabs was open plan with a reasonable sized garden at the rear, along with an Anderson shelter which did service as a shed/coal bunker during peace time.

Each of these bungalows was constructed with an outer face of prefabricated asbestos panels bolted to a galvanized steel frame; a practice which would be frowned upon today, but it didn't matter so much in those days. In the centre of the front wall, floor to roof, was a large galvanized steel panel, which encompassed the front door and outer walls of the toilet and bathroom. This steel panel was painted by the council every few years, each prefab a different (and quite garish) colour. I remember ours once was a very bright orange. People from the

Mary Baker's childhood home in Hamilton Avenue.

surrounding area often referred to the prefab estate as 'Toy Town' but we didn't care, we liked our houses.

J. Imhof

Mutton stew

We lived on stews mainly. Horrible greasy mutton stew or bones boiled up with vegetables. We were lucky and had some blackcurrant bushes so Mum bottled these and we had pies occasionally. There were no eggs except some in an earthenware jar preserved in something. Butter was very sparse. Bread and dripping was the norm.

Pat Owers

Games

We played cards quite a bit. We would go to our neighbours every other Saturday and play solo with them. With our girls we played all sorts of board games. In fact, we still have most of them: dominos, cribbage and monopoly. Our grandchildren although grown up have memories of coming to Grandma and Granddad and playing games.

Ron Ketteridge

Christmas

When we were kids at Christmas we just had a stocking, which was one of my Dad's long socks. As the material wasn't open weave, you didn't know what you had got until you emptied it out on to your bed. My sister, being more feminine than I, received dolls and dolls clothes. I was more of a tomboy so had teddy bears and all the annuals – *Beano*, *Dandy* and *Rupert*. You then opened your stocking and there were usually perhaps a few nuts, and if you were lucky, fruit or something like that. They were like gold dust when I was a kid.

Linda Reside

Money in the pot

There was one person in the street who owned a car. Usually it was the same person who had a phone. They would expect people to go along and ask to use it. You made your call then put some money in the pot at the side. You only used it in an emergency, nobody ever took advantage.

Mary Baker (*née* Lawrence)

Rag-and-bone sacks

The rag-and-bone man would come regularly. We had two sacks that hung in the scullery, one for rags and one for bones. When he came round if I got tuppence or fourpence for them I was allowed to keep it.

D. Williams

Dapper

I remember having my photo taken whilst walking down Tomswood Hill. I was going out for the day. In those days I had a suit on which was a classy brown and white chalk

Mary Baker's (*née* Lawrence) family in Hamilton Avenue.

stripe, a collar, tie and a pair of kid gloves. I was only young as I hadn't left school long. It was a boiling hot day and I remember a couple of kids running past and said 'Look at him, got gloves on.' I took those gloves off, stuffed them in my pocket and never wore them again. The suit cost a shilling a week to buy off the tallyman.

Len Smith

Stag beetle alert

I developed a keen interest in the flora and fauna, regularly contributing to the school nature table. We had dozens of stag beetles which used to fly over Station Approach during May and June. We would catch them and I kept one large individual male about two-and-a-half inches long as a pet. I took it to school in the top pocket of my blazer and when my Mum collected me we went shopping to Dyson's with my friend Ann's mum. I asked her if she would like to see my new pet and she innocently agreed. I opened my pocket and out marched this huge beetle. Poor Mary screamed and alerted by the shriek all the other lady shoppers turned to look. There followed a stampede for the door. I think it cleared the shop in roughly thirty seconds. After a clip round the ear, the stag beetles were no longer allowed out on excursions.

Carol Baldwin

Tin chapel

We originally went to the tiny old Methodist chapel in the High Street. It was called the Tin chapel although built of brick, not tin. It was roughly where Choice is now. When that was pulled down the first library was put up. The Methodist church then moved to its place in Freemantle Road.

Ron Ketteridge

Our house in New North Road

There were two medium-sized bedrooms, my parents had one and my sisters and I shared the other. My brother had a small box room. The house in Barkingside seemed enormous after our cottage. I suppose that is why I grew up always thinking of it as a large house. In fact, when I saw it as an adult, it was disappointingly small. The wood yard which joined our house was on the corner of Trelawney Road.

Jean Westbeech (*née* Thompson)

Errands

I can remember being sent on errands by my mother to Mr Cook the butcher in Cranbrook Road near to Hamilton Avenue. I would get three-quarter ounce rump steak. My favourite lunch was sausages and tomatoes. I also liked rice pudding with evaporated milk or condensed sweetened milk and bananas. Came the war and you couldn't get a banana.

John Baker

Carol Baldwin, *c*. 1960.

seven
The High Street

H-Bone

Mother would walk down one side of the High Street stopping at the butchers where she would point to a carcass of beef hanging in the window and ask for an H-bone roast to be cut. The butcher would unhook the meat throw it on his wooden bench and use a cleaver to chop off the part she wanted, then as quick as lightening take a sharp knife and trim and roll and string the meat up and wrap it in white butcher paper.

Patricia Lange (*née* Dawson)

Broadway Parade

There were a few shops at the bottom of the road. A newsagent/confectioner, a shoe repairer, draper's and Green's stores which was also a post office. The post office had a telephone in the shop, so if the shop was closed it was necessary to go either to Fairlop station or to the Chequers to telephone. On the corner was Chatter's coal yard and they had a sweet shop too. Eventually when the new shops were built Chatter's came up to Tomswood Hill (opposite Colvin Gardens) and they had a sweet shop in a shed. The shops built on Chatter's yard were Wakeman's the grocer and Forge's the sweet shop. I think there was also a butcher.

M. Ellis

How things change

The shops have changed so much in the High Street. On one side of Frank Norman's was a half shop, which sold washing powders and household cleaning items. Then there was Goodrich the ironmongers and a large Co-op selling clothes. Next to Frank Norman's on the other side was Home and Colonial grocers, then Sketchley the cleaners with a stocking repair machine to mend ladders. Joyce was the manageress. She was a very kind lady and friend. Then there was Forest's shoe repairers. Opposite was a café, a poodle parlour and Jenner's, which sold all sorts of linens and clothes. Mrs Cook owned the wool shop. One Christmas she knitted me a beautiful jumper as a present (wool wasn't easy to get in those days). We must not forget Marment's where children loved to go and look at the toys, hoping to get one for Christmas.

E. Kemble

Onion men

I can remember the largest shop was the Co-op. Tesco, only little like a corner shop but self-service with two aisles, was by the library. Fifty Shilling Tailors was a large gents' outfitter. There was also a greenhouse which sold flowers and fruit opposite Barkingside Recreation Ground. At the bottom of Tomswood Hill, near the Maypole, was United Dairies milk distribution centre. It had a cobbled entrance and stables for the horses. The Co-op also had horse-drawn milk carts and our milkman was called George. His horse was named Foxhunter after the Olympic star. I used to earn pocket money helping out

Greetings from Barkingside, c. 1950.

delivering milk whilst George called in for numerous cups of tea, or so he said. Bread and cakes were delivered to your door by Barton's bakery, and ice creams in large churns on box bikes were a common sight before modern vans. Other vendors were the French onion men on bikes with onions draped around necks and over handlebars and a guy with a bicycle-powered grinder who sharpened knives and scissors.

Ray Burton

Local tradesmen

We had the coalman delivering the coal. I can remember the shellfish van and having winkles for Sunday tea. They would park up and we would go out and buy the shellfish. I can also recall the electric floats, and Hitchman's the milkman who had the dairy in the High Street.

Ann Reed

Ticket to Skegness

The corner shop at Horace Road was a strange shop called Swainson's. It was principally a confectioner's and tobacconist's but it also sold rail tickets. At the back of the shop were wooden shelves with small compartments containing stacks of small pink card train tickets. We never bought train tickets as my family never travelled anywhere by train, but there were rail posters advertising exotic places to visit (where on earth was Skegness?) and I wanted to go and root about in the stacks of tickets just to see what was there. I never did, of course, and it was a shop we seldom went into, but I would have loved to go in and buy four tickets to Skegness.

Derek Lawrence

Dinner for a shilling

All the shops in Barkingside were empty units when the war came. They sandbagged them up and if there was an air raid you just dived into one of them. We had the Roosevelt Restaurant (at the end of the post office block at Westminster Gardens). It would have been about two whole shops. Although it was sandbagged up outside, inside it was decorated with murals on the wall and you could get a dinner for a shilling.

Irene Vaughan

Deliveries in the 1930s

Milk was delivered by horse and cart before breakfast and also later in the morning. The United Dairies cart was bright orange and the horse knew each house where it should stop. There was also daily delivery of bread by a small handcart with two handles for the baker to pull it along.

M. Ellis

Green's Stores

I recall Green's stores was in the parade of shops almost opposite the Fairlop Oak. The shop sold provisions and was convenient if you did not want to venture into Barkingside High Street. I remember Mossford Garage in the High Street on the corner now where Somerfield's supermarket is. I can also picture Wallis' which I believe was a grocer near to the end of the High Street.

Rose Dean

Famous ice cream

All I can remember of Barkingside High Street itself was a park and Rossi's famous ice-cream parlour.

Roy St Pierre

Flour at the State

There were several empty shops in the High Street which were used to store food during the war. They had big wooden doors on them with padlocks. In the State cinema they stored flour and I can remember seeing men wheeling out big white sacks and loading them onto lorries. The rumour went round that the cinema was alive with rats. The ARP hut was near Broadway Parade – this was later knocked down and the new toilets built.

Alison Bush (*née* Dryborough)

Whelam's

Whelam's was in Tanners Lane. It was a small half shop with shelves littered with jars of sweets. You could see right through to the back of the shop, which seemed to be a

Ann Reed (*née* Croft) aged eight, with her mother.

living room of sorts. It didn't sell papers as I remember but sold all types of tobacco and cigars. At Easter you could buy Suchard eggs which when broken in half each egg had a different filling. I would by two ounces of floral gums if I was lucky, which many of my friends hated and called soap sweets. You could also buy coconut tobacco consisting of a very sweet brown sugary coating over large strips of coconut. It took ages to chew.

H. Kemble

Sainsbury's

The High Street was the main food shopping area and some of the shops I remember were Pither's bakery, Eastwell's the greengrocers, Rossi and Sainsbury's, which took up two shops. Not at all like the Sainsbury's we know today. Each department had a separate counter that was not dissimilar to the delicatessen, butcher and fish counters in today's modern supermarkets. One had to queue at each counter for your produce. The butter was also sold loose and butter pats (two pieces of wood shaped like a bat) were used to shape it into the oblong shapes we would recognise today.

Hazel Pudney

Alderman Green

Green' stores at Broadway Parade was the grocers, a family firm. Alderman Green was Mayor and quite an important person in Ilford.

Ron Ketteridge

Redmond's

I liked Redmond's sweet shop but the sweets were on ration. As they knew me I managed to get a little bit extra. You couldn't get much of an assortment but my favourites were Love

Hearts and bags of Butterkist. When rations finished I liked liquorice comfits, allsorts and aniseed balls. My first bike came from Kingsway Sports and had drop handlebars. I cycled with a friend and went as far as Dunmow and Fyfield. I would be worried cycling now.

Ann Reed (*née* Croft)

Magical ingredient

Before our local shops up Fencepiece Road were built, we had to regularly visit the High Street for our weekly shopping. As Eastertide approached we would visit Pither's the bakers. Baking was still done on the premises so it was the only source of yeast. No dried yeast in those days. My mother always made her own hot-cross buns so needed the yeast. I was fascinated that this grey putty-like stuff was such a vital magical ingredient. Pither's baked delicious bread, including the Hovis rolls, miniatures of the Hovis loaf.

Faye Pedder

Six and seven-eighths

When we came to Barkingside there was a men's outfitter near to HSBC. I would walk down there before the war with my father and he would always wear a cap, size six and seven-eighths. He would walk in and ask for a new cap, the shopkeeper would only ask what colour and bring a box down onto the counter. The first one out of the box was the right size.

Irene Vaughan

Boots made to measure

Crawley, the boot maker, lived in a cottage in the High Street and had a shop round the back in the alleyway. Once a year I would go round there and get my feet measured and he

High Street, Barkingside, (note the Hovis sign outside the baker's on the right) 1950s.

would make me a pair of boots and tell that it would cost my father five shillings. They were all handmade and comfortable. When he moved out from there he went down New North Road and still carried on repairing in his garage.

Len Smith

Big shop

When I was very young before Manford Way shops were built we either walked to Grange Hill or Hainault to shop. Once a week we did a big shop in Barkingside. My mother would push my younger brother in a pushchair and if I got tired I was allowed to stand on the footboard. Before we crossed over at the State roundabout there was a hobbies shop that had an electric train set up in the window, with a slot for you to put in a penny to make it go.

Patricia Lange (née Dawson)

Ice treat

In the High Street there was Rossi ice-cream parlour and when we got our pay once a month my friend and I would go up and have a pineapple sundae. We would get paid £2 14s

a month. I also went to a dentist who was up in the High Street and I had four impacted wisdom teeth out there, two at a time, and when I came back to work I had to go back on duty again and give the children their tea.

Kathy Alston

The Old High Street

Before the war, all this area was a country village more or less and there weren't many people. Barkingside High Street started to be built up, first on the right - and then on the left-hand side.

Roy Wilkinson

Everything you need

We walked along to Sainsbury's first with its wonderful descriptive tiles. Eggs (after the war) came in paper bags. I lost count of just how many we broke. One egg would break and soak the bag then all the rest would fall out. Butter was shaped with butter-beaters. We used to get our tiny 2ozs. Then to queue again for bacon or meat, often fly blown. From here we went to Telmer's store. Boxes and boxes of biscuits,

CHIGWELL ROW CHURCH

HAINAULT FOREST

HAINAULT

MANFORD WAY

THE LAKE, HAINAULT FOREST

GRANGE HILL, CHIGWELL

Greetings from
Hainault, c. 1950.

tea in tea chests, sugar in bins. We usually bought ¼lb of loose tea in a brown bag, ½lb of sugar in a blue bag and ½lb broken biscuits in a brown paper bag. Sometimes we went into Goodriche's and bought candles. Next was Woolworths. It was very dark in there and I didn't like it. We bought nutmegs at ¼p each. We stopped at Gurr's the fishmongers for a cod head for the cat – it was huge in those days. Crossing to Pither's bakery we bought one-penny buns to eat at home. Coming back with weary legs we used the large pram to store shopping under the panels in the pram where my younger sister and brother sat.

Pat Owers

Balls and old rackets

I was born and lived with my family in Oak Row, which is approximately where Woolworths now stands. The cottages were later condemned as they were right on the main road and you only had a short garden. We had to be re-housed and eventually settled in Kingsley Road. On the corner where the swimming pool is now was Mr Phillips' saw mill where he would cut up firewood. In front

was a pond. His horse would drink from it. If it were a bit dirty it would find a piece of paper to drink through as horses won't drink dirty water. Alongside of that, going towards Barkingside was a pavilion and tennis courts. We would go in there and play a game of snooker and have a cup of tea. I would get under the pavilion and find balls and old rackets. Part of the Fairlop fair was always on the corner there.

Len Smith

Favourite shops

I used to love Barkingside High Street. We had a lovely diverse selection of shops which included, Jenner's drapers, Wallis' supermarket, Pollard's clothes shop, Eastwell's greengrocers and many more. My favourites were Pets beauty parlour and the little shop just round the corner in Fencepiece Road near our doctor's, which sold models and had a model railway running round its window which you put money in a slot outside to operate. I used to be allowed this treat when I was ill, and actually enjoyed going to see Dr Franklin.

Carol Baldwin

Left: Barkingside High Street, 1951, looking from Baron Gardens towards where Oak Row once was.

Below: Fred in Tucker's butchers, where Carol Baldwin worked.

Posh nosh

In the seventies and eighties there was a Sainsbury's Freezer Centre at the end of the High Road and you could walk through it to get to the Sainsbury's store behind. We would also feel posh eating in High Tide on a Saturday evening. Everyone else seemed to have takeaways.

Amanda Ross

Squashy tomatoes and boiling beet

I recall the days when you could walk down the High Street and the shop windows advertised for Saturday staff. I didn't fancy Barton's the bakers and got a job at Eastwell's greengrocers. The fruit and vegetable counters were separate sides of the double fronted shop. You had to master the vegetables, old till and scales before being allowed to serve on the fruit counter. The Eastwell family were well known in Barkingside and owned a couple of other shops. Local people shopped there and it was nice to be familiar with the customers who came in every week. Everything was put in brown paper bags that hung on string. Squashy tomatoes were sold at a reduced price and beetroot was cooked by Eric, in a boiler out the back of the shop. At Christmas, trees were sold and it was great fun trying to put a rather large tree into a potato sack. Working Christmas Eve made it feel an extra special time. Unfortunately supermarkets have taken over the independent retailer. I was sorry to see shops like this disappear.

H. Kemble

Avis

Our radio had an accumulator battery, which we had to take to Avis in Mossford Green for charging quite often. I never used the telephone until 1950 when I took my Brownie badge. I inserted four old pennies and pushed button A. You then dialled, I think, and if there was no reply you pressed button B and your money came back.

Pat Owers

eight

Here and There

The Stall

Near the Maypole in Fencepiece Road, before the shops were built, used to be spare ground with lumps and bumps. It was good to go on your bike. On the corner of the piece of waste ground there used to be a little place called The Stall. It was a trestle table with canvas round it and hurricane lamps, selling potatoes and greens. I would come home from school and if my mum had run out of potatoes she would ask me to go down the stall and get her some. I had a three-wheeled bike with a tin on the back which had a lid. I would scoot down there on my three-wheeled bike and get her the greens and potatoes and put them in the tin box at the back.

Linda Reside

Newbury Park and the Fairlop Loop

Newbury Park was part of the Fairlop Loop. Looking at the lack of development at the time, one would wonder what the demand was, but it is clear that a massive housing complex was planned south of what is now Eastern Avenue – then simply Hatch Lane. There was a complex of sidings at Newbury Park in my childhood. I remember the coal shunting during the night. Steam trains were used there in to the 1960s. I also recall having to visit the coal office that stood just outside the station.

The idea of the Fairlop Loop was to link Seven Kings to the Ongar branch at Woodford. Indeed on a map it is shown as the Woodford and Ilford Branch. The plans to make the line part of London Underground's Central Line network were laid in 1936 but work wasn't complete until 1948. The tunnels, however, from Wanstead to Newbury Park were in place so that they could be used for aircraft part production. In the Second World War Plessey's had a factory two-and-half-miles long. The present frontage to the station is a Grade II listed building. The original concept nearly failed. It was planned as far back as 1897 and Barkingside station boasted the glory of a Baroque cupola and weather vane on its roof. But trams were seen as having a greater future and in the race to open, the trams won. The tramway from Ilford to Barkingside opened six weeks before the railway and train passengers were almost non-existent. Later still the future for the line seemed brighter yet because Fairlop was seriously considered as the site for London's airport, but Heathrow was of course eventually chosen.

I have reason to be grateful for the Central Line. My late parent's house was in easy walking distance.

Geoffrey Gillon

Walking

We walked from Ilford through Valentines Park into Gants Hill and always walked from Hainault to Barkingside to school. We would not have dreamt of getting the bus. It was about three quarters of a mile. We had no money for the bus anyway.

Amanda Ross

Gravel pit

During the war in Aldborough Hatch in Oaks Lane there was a recreation ground and it was the first gravel pit, to my knowledge, on Hainault Plain. It was excavated before the war and it was open, left with water and unfenced. After Sunday school my brother, sister and I would go along there and play on the gravel pits. One particular day I fell in. There was a sheer drop into the water and my brother had to fish me out.

Ron Jeffries

Barnardo's hospital

We had three months' training in the hospital. It was a lovely place. They had two doctors, Dr Bloom and Dr Bywaters. They could treat all minor illnesses. Obviously if the children had infectious diseases, such as measles or mumps, they had to go into the hospital.

Kathy Alston

Robert's Circus

Robert's Circus would sometimes use the piece of ground where the library is. Later they had the circus on the waste ground at Fowler's Farm, which is now called Forest Farm.

Ron Ketteridge

Princess Margaret

One summer in the sixties, before I left Grange County high school, people were all talking about the new boys club that had been built and were saying someone famous was coming to open it. Sure enough a helicopter landed on the high school field and Princess Margaret stepped out. Police were there trying to hold back the crowd. I was there with my brother Anthony and he edged forward and snapped a picture.

Patricia Lange (*née* Dawson)

Dipping Horns Road

Horns Road still has a big dip in it. This was where the Cranbrook River used to run through. It was like a small ford in the road. It was eventually piped in.

Ray Ross

Pigswill

As I grew older my forays took me further afield. I would be taken for walks to our local farm run by Mr and Mrs Lewis. Mum would buy eggs and then we would go and see the pigs. Huge great white spotted creatures of uncertain temper. The pungent stink of their swill being cooked in the pig boiler can still be recalled. Sometimes I was allowed to go in a sty and see the newborn piglets. The farm also had wild cats. The pig man told me if I could catch one I could keep it. I had as much chance of catching a cloud. Those little spitting balls of fury moved like lightening. I spent many an hour trying.

Carol Baldwin

Spilling down the hill

I have no idea what its proper name was. In fact, that may have been it. We reached it by a long walk down Fullwell Avenue to where

HRH Princess Margaret arriving at Grange School 1960s.

Gilbert Colvin School, Class 4T, *c*. 1958.

that road then petered out in a mess of rubble in a field. There were the remains of a fence to be got through or further broken and, then, we were there. The hill may not have been very impressive; the name suggests it was hardly a great eminence. You could not see it until you got pretty close, but it was good enough for us.

We used to drag our soap-box carts over there. These were boards with pram wheels attached and makeshift steering systems. The only soap-boxes I have ever seen are made of cardboard and would not be of the slightest use in making carts. Half the fun was that you were unlikely to get to the bottom of the hill without an exhilarating spill. Even a relatively timid boy, like me, got a lot of fun out of our hectic downhill races. The winner was invariably the one who stayed aboard ongest. Faster usually meant an early upset. No-one had prepared the track by removing bumps, tussocks, projecting stones and roots or smoothed away the rather corrugated structure of one part of the slope.

Getting home was often a real bind. If the cart had been damaged, which was certainly not rare, it had to be carried. This was worse the farther it had to be carried. I lived in Jerningham Avenue, more than a mile away on

the other side of a ridge. The top of the ridge was Belvedere Avenue, where our school, Gilbert Colvin, was situated.

Roger O'Brien

New North Road

New North Road was not as it is today but even in the 1930s there were pavements and a tarmac road surface, all quite strange to the kids from the Edmonton sticks. Directly opposite our house there was a large factory, Kelvin Hughes. Most of the activity in the road was the coming and going of the men who worked in the factory. I remember watching them through a knothole in the high wooden fence at the front of the house and garden.

Jean Westbeech (née Thompson)

Hainault Move and *Comic Cuts*

I was born in Romford but came to live at No. 6 New North Road. It was one of the cottages up by the Old Hainault Oak. There was a big wooden building at the side; an alley went up and round the corner to these cottages. I remember they had black tar wood on them. The little local shops would deliver. The van had oval windows in the back and I would always look for that when he arrived with my comic, *Comic Cuts*. The two characters were Weary Willy and Tired Tim along with a German spy with all moustaches sticking out – the evil one.

Charles Ernest Winter

Thunderbolt

On Thursday 31 May 1972, at about 6 o'clock in the evening we had a freak storm. There was torrential rain and suddenly a terrific bang. I was getting dinner ready for my family. The telephone was cut off; the television shook and went off. I couldn't believe what was happening. Our youngest daughter was so frightened I could not leave her so was unable to go upstairs to find out what had happened. Our eldest daughter's future mother-in-law, who lived across the way, came round to see if we were alright. She had seen a thunderbolt strike houses two away from ours. We were very lucky it missed our house, but we hadn't escaped any damage. It had knocked our chimney down, which had fallen on to our conservatory causing the roof to be destroyed. The rain was pouring through. When my husband and daughter arrived home from work they were shocked to see the police, fire brigade and ambulance there. Fortunately, nobody was hurt. The worst thing for us was that our eldest daughter was getting married in ten days' time so we had to get it repaired very quickly. I must say that is something that I will never forget and every time there is a storm now I make sure everything is turned off and stay downstairs and away from the conservatory.

E. Kemble

The pirate bus

At the bottom of the road where Tomswood Hill adjoins Fencepiece Road was the Old Maypole and the General Buses from Ilford stopped there. Fares to Ilford were 3d. There was also a pirate bus, cost to Ilford 2d. It was later that the Old Maypole was moved near New North Road.

M. Ellis

Fishing at Forest Road

We didn't venture much up Lambourne End but we used to go up Manford Way before it was built on in the 1950s. It was all open land and we would often go down that way to the

Grey Goose Cottage, Fullwel, *c.* 1900.

lake at Hainault for night fishing. At the end of the 1940s we would fish where the transport place is now in Forest Road. There was a big lake and a willow tree, which is still there.

Bert Reed

Cheeky mouse

During the war my aunt had a cheeky little mouse that lived behind the skirting by her fireplace — a nice warm spot for him as coal fires were lit. He would venture out and became quite bold in front of anyone in the room. During the winter we'd scrape the ice off the inside of the bedroom windows, and the feather eiderdowns everyone had then were needed greatly.

Sheila Dorling (*née* Smith)

Ripping ride on the 275

In the early 1980s, the old fashioned buses with rear stairs and conductor still ran on the 275. I jumped off the back of the bus at traffic lights at Walthamstow market and ripped a hole in my trousers when the bus pulled off and I fell into the road. Another time I dared a young bus driver to drive round the Barkingside roundabout twice. This he did and everyone on the top deck fell off the seats. He would have lost his job in today's world.

Amanda Ross

Homemade Olympics

We had great fun over Valentines Park having sports competitions with friends. We were all around fifteen or sixteen years old.

Faulkner family photograph (Sheila Dorling's mother is seated).

The park had a pitch and putt, which we frequently played but we also made up our own games. Tossing the brick represented the shot put; throwing the bean cane, the javelin and running round the cricket pitch, the mile. Our medals were made from the tops of orange bottles. Red for first, green for second and yellow for third.

Other games we played at home were Gobstones (or five stones), marbles and knock down ginger. We would also flick cigarette cards against the wall. Another pastime was collecting lollypop sticks.

Brian Taylor

Magnificent buses

The trolleybuses! Who could forget those magnificent quiet purveyors of people? I was told as a child that they were originally built to be sent to South Africa and that was why they had tinted glass. The war came so they did not go but provided a service between Barkingside and Barking instead. Running on electric cables overhead, the 691 as it was then, was so different to the noisy diesel-guzzling beasts. Such a pity we no longer have them – much more ecologically friendly. Sometimes an arm would come off the overhead wires and it would have to wait for a man to arrive with a pointy stick to get the arm back and the trolleybus could resume its majestic course.

Faye Pedder

Trotter's Field

Up at Trotter's Field, round the back of the Retreat public house in Chigwell Row was a big shed that didn't have a bar in it but had seats, tables and a piano. That is where we used to go and Bob Kemble would play the piano.

Irene Vaughan

Manford Way shopping

The shops at Manford Way came quite some while after the estate because the vans used to come round and deliver. One I can remember was Lipton's who delivered groceries and vegetables. There was once a Sainsbury's and Bennett's the newsagents and a few more shops along the other end of Manford Way where Grange Hill station is. A newsagents in a hut by the side of the railway where the children would take their old comics, getting one new one for two older ones and on the other side by the railway there was Rowena Nurseries and Enever's, a little shop that sold sweets. It also had little tables at the back for teas. Mr and Mrs Enever came to my twins' christening at All Saints church at Chigwell Row, opposite the Maypole.

Harriet Dawson

Disappearing gardens

In the 1950s, Forest Road was little more than a country lane. The road was made, the only pavement being on the side of Fairlop station. I have noticed the increase in traffic since I retired twenty-one years ago and also how front gardens have disappeared – they are a thing of the past

Ron Ketteridge

Brownies and dance troupe

I remember I went on holiday to Worthing with the Brownie Pack from Gants Hill Methodist church where, incidentally, I later became Brown Owl. Also in the 1950s I was in a dance troupe. We would put on displays, some of which were at Claybury Hospital, for the patients.

Hazel Pudney

Dance troupe display at
Claybury, 1955.

Gants Hill Methodist Brownie
pack trip, c. 1950.

The Wright Brothers

Before the war two brothers, Billy and Wally Wright, cultivated the field behind our house in Fencepiece Road. The field was backing on to what is now Trelawney Road. They had a big shire horse and a plough and you could hear them shouting 'Giddy up boy'. All of us kids used to go up there putting cabbages in the ground for them. They would plod the holes and we put the seed cabbages in. We would also help with potato and pea picking.

The Wright brothers lived in some cottages down Horns Road, just past the Horns Tavern. They let me sit on the back of the shire horse from Fencepiece Road all the way down the lane where Craven Gardens is now, pulling a cart, and when we got to the stable they let me undo the horse from the cart, drive him into his stable and brush him down with one of those big brushes. Upstairs they had a big machine. You had to put the old hay on it and as it came along you turned a big wheel and cut it into chaff, which would be put in the nosebag. I could then feed him. They also had a scoop with a big tin of oats and they would tell me to give him only half a scoop, but I used to give him one that was nearly full and the horse used to look at me and I am sure he used to wink! Pals we were, that horse and me.

Roy Wilkinson

Fairlop Oak looking towards Broadway Parade, *c. 1930.*

Local landmarks

We didn't have cars so, as a family, we cycled everywhere. All over Essex, out to Brentwood, Ongar and beyond. There weren't any signposts during the war as these had been removed, so we would go by the pubs as landmarks, for example, turn left at the Maypole, straight on by the Beehive. I still use these as landmarks today.

Ron Jeffries

Welsh miners

I attended Gants Hill Methodist church and before the war we had a Welsh Minister. All the miners were out of work so he invited some of them up and everyone in the church invited one of them home and looked after them for a while. They were genuinely poor people. I remember they had beautiful singing voices. Some even kept in touch with them after they went back.

Mary Baker (*née* Lawrence)

Over the bumps

Across the road from the Ilford County High in Freemantle Road was a piece of waste ground that was subsequently built upon. It was seldom I would travel on my tricycle as far as that but occasionally I accompanied my mum to the High Street. It was drummed into me that under no circumstances was I to attempt to cross the 'busy' Clayhall Avenue. 'Busy'? A 129 bus every twenty minutes and the Corona fizzy drink delivery van once a week. Sometimes I went out following my elder (by six years) brother on his bicycle. Not often was I allowed too close – after all, what about his street cred, but just sometimes we headed for this wondrous land of excitement. There were large bumps and dips I did not know but they provided fast freewheels down-wards and sliding climbs up the other side. Often puddles of muddy water at the bottom of the hollows added to the excitement as we must not get mud on our clothes. So, feet high in the air as you went through a puddle and ride through the puddles on the way home to get the mud off the tyres.

Derek Lawrence

Flying saucers

At the bottom of Tomswood Hill there was a little row of very old cottages, probably from the 1800s, and one of those little cottages was turned into a tiny café and we would buy our sweets there. At one time you could get eight blackjacks for a penny. We used to buy great big blocks of honeycomb that would make your teeth go funny and sherbet dabs, sherbet fountains and flying saucers that were rice paper with sherbet in the middle. If you bit them and took too much of an intake of breath the sherbet ended up coming down your nose.

Linda Reside

Manford Way FC

The club name is after the main road that runs from Manor Road near Grange Hill station to Hainault Forest on the Romford Road through the Hainault Estate. The Club was founded in 1946 when Harry Rumsey and Bill Wright formed the 1st Manford Way Team, then known as the Chigwell Labour Club, for one season. The name was then officially changed to Manford Way FC. Bill Wright was club Secretary, a position which he held until I took over in 1975 until 1999. The club has enjoyed many successful seasons in various divisions. Its current home ground is at the LPR sports ground in Forest Road, Hainault. Harry Rumsey is now in his nineties and still lives in the area. Unfortunately Bill Wright died six or more years ago after retiring to Norfolk. I am now the current president.

T. Cove

Savage's

I would go to the local nursery; Savage's in Fencepiece Road, where I bought freshly picked tomatoes, lettuce and other vegetables. There was a fabulous stall on the field by the old Maypole pub where you bought strawberries in the summer. This field went for the shops to be built.

Pat Owers

Coal at Newbury Park

In my childhood, I remember there was a complex of sidings at Newbury Park. During the night coal shunting could be heard. I also recall having to visit the coal office which stood just outside the station.

Geoffrey Gillon

Safe to shop

When one of my daughters was about eight, I would let her go down Forest Road to Broadway Market. There were grocers, chemist, greengrocer and butchers on this side of the road. You wouldn't let a child do that by itself now. Most of the shops changed when the supermarkets were built.

Marjorie Ketteridge

The Buntingbridge

Where we lived in Birkbeck Road was on the corner of Abbey Road and that ran down in the cul-de-sac. Down the bottom was the brook called the Buntingbridge and we would go down there and pick watercress. There was a big water pipe the size of a motor steering wheel which ran right the way along, and as children we would walk along it balancing. When I visited recently we drove over it in the car as there are houses built there and it had all been filled in.

D. Williams

Boys' County High. Freemantle Road, opposite waste ground where art lessons took place. Flats have now been built on this area.

Waste ground art lessons

Opposite the Boys County High where the flats now are, was wasteland where old carts and things were dumped. We would be taken over there sometimes for art lessons and have to draw the things that we could see on the wasteland.

Ron Ketteridge

Changing places

I remember when Somerfield was Key Markets; the new Sainsbury's was So-colds which you could get to from Chase Lane. Tescos' was Barnardo's and Timberdene was part of Claybury fields. Claybury was a hospital and not full of 'des-res' homes. Claybury hospital chapel is now a swimming pool.

Amanda Ross

Gaysham's

I was told that the houses in Gaysham Avenue were built for the PLA and having built them, the PLA being in London, realised it was too far for them to travel. They sold them on the open market. That was where the original Gaysham Hall land was.

Mary Baker (*née* Lawrence)

Swimming at Grange Farm

I remember as child going to Grange Farm. It was in Chigwell and had a swimming pool. In fact we had our swimming lessons there from school. There were also wide-open spaces for plenty of recreation.

Linda Barnes (*née* Cove)

Travelling to Barkingside

I didn't ever live in Barkingside, my home being in Goodmayes but I did go to the grammar school there. It involved two bus journeys and I remember walking the three miles every day during the great smog of 1957. We had swimming lessons at Ilford Baths and used to get a trolleybus along Horns Road and Ley Street. Later the school had its own swimming pool built. I do remember that every year when the fifth year left the school they got up to pranks. The most wild of these was somehow getting a teacher's car up on a flat roof of an outbuilding. One of my brothers also embarrassed me by marrying my geography master's daughter. During his lessons we would have our atlas's upright on the desks busily doing our French homework. The strange thing was the whole class did really well at our Geography GCE. I think we must all have panicked about the subject and over-compensated by revising like mad. I only received the cane once and that was for the dreadful crime of selling stamps in the dinner hour as I was an avid collector.

Roy St Pierre

nine
Village Life

Plenty to do

There was always lots to do during the summer holidays. We would picnic and swim at Grange Farm, taking the footpath at Grange Hill through the farmer's fields to Chigwell and walk up the road passing the Old King's Head. Blackberry picking at the Hainault lake was another favourite outing or just to playing fields at Chigwell Row for a picnic tea.

Patricia Lange (*née* Dawson)

Patricia Lange with her siblings, Hainault Forest outing, 1953.

Rafting on the Roding

One memory is of the river Roding, which was reached by a march further past Pancake Hill. The Roding is not a major stream. I should think it could be waded safely in Wellies at most times of the year. However, there was one time when we decided to venture out on it. We made a raft in my back garden by nailing planks together. Because of the distance to the Roding we made the raft in six sections, which were to be nailed together on the riverbank.

My old cart was the means of dragging raft sections, bag of nails, hammer and a good deal of spare wood all the way to the Roding. It was a hot day and a long drag. At length, we got there and lugged the sections off the cart and into position. I seem to remember this bit going rather well. We assembled the raft in very good time. Dragging it down to the water's edge was not too bad, because we had assembled it close by. However, one inch of water did not support the raft. We dragged it in a bit farther. Two inches of water did not support it. We studied the problem. One end was still firmly land-bound and, exerting considerable leverage on the part in the water, we dragged and pushed it a lot farther until even the bank-ward side was in two inches of water. I put a tentative foot on the raft, which promptly grounded on the riverbed. I jumped back and we made sure that the whole thing was floating. Well, 'floating' is a bit strong. It wallowed with the connecting struts just out of the water, but the actual sections

Spicer's Cottages in Hainault Road.

under the surface. The sluggish current did not move it at all. Minnows investigated it. We manoeuvred the thing out into mid-stream, all of fifteen feet from the edge of the water. Given some rain and plenty of time, I suppose the raft might have floated all the way down to the Thames at Barking Creek. In fact, it may have done so eventually. The problem was that it would not carry a passenger heavier than a half brick so we abandoned it and our dreams of navigation and went home. I can't remember whether it was lunch or tea we returned to. We did take the cart with us, in case that did turn out to be useful for something else.

Dad reckoned that we had used so many nails in the construction of the raft that their weight nearly sank it. He did manage to keep a straight face as he explained this.

Roger O'Brien

Hainault Road cottages

My grandfather, Fred Spicer, owned cottages in Hainault Road – on the right-hand side if travelling towards Barley Lane. The cottages still remain and don't seem to have changed much at all.

Jackie Spicer

Laying out the locals

The fragile economic status of the Victorian working class ensured that tough women like Alice Dance and her daughter, Fanny Knight (*née* Dance), were there to perform a much-needed role in North Ilford society. During the final decades of Queen Victoria's reign and the early decades of the twentieth century, undertakers would have failed to make a living from working-class families. Raising large families throughout the town, from the Cauliflowers [pub] in the south, to the Horns [pub] in the north, neighbours relied on Alice and Fanny. Calling upon them to help prepare departed loved ones for their final journey; initially, to have them layed out. Alice had taught Fanny this necessary neighbourly chore in Barkingside,

Fanny Knight with her eight children (Fanny is on the right, in front of bride).

solving an unavoidable final problem for the folk there that the restraints of poverty put upon them. A legacy of those deprived days, today many graves of ex-Freehold residents are unknown. Any passing away occurring on the Freehold, Birkbeck Road, Perrymans Farm Road, Abbey Road and the like involved contacting Fanny Knight first. The last journey to an unused spot in the burial ground around St Peter's church at Aldborough Hatch, without this help from Fanny, was unthinkable and unaffordable. Final resting places there, afterwards, often remained unmarked.

Through her nursing service in the girls' home in Barkingside, Fanny became even more invaluable to friends, family and neighbours in the clan that was the Freehold. On one memorable Christmas day Fanny was called to care for one of her ailing 'old' people. This involved leaving her own very large family gathered round trestle tables singing together to Bert's upright piano playing in their two-up two-down in Netley Road. Fanny then was nearly eighty and the 'old' patient? She was almost sixty-five!

Like so many of her 'customers' before her Fanny's name was not to be etched on marble-stone at her passing. Not, that is, until her grateful grandchildren gathered to admire the stonemason's new work rectifying this omission in the shade of St Peter's church, on 6 December 2003, the 109th anniversary of her birthday. Fanny Knight, like many others of the Freehold's era neither expected nor received acknowledgement or awards in her lifetime. Service then was expected and freely offered. No trestle table or upright piano at that happy gathering at her graveside in 2003, just honour restored and bags of pride.

Brynley Knight (grandson)

Gants Hill

Gants Hill was where we went to the Odeon cinema. We also changed buses there for Leyton County High. Valentines Park in that area was a beautiful park. In my courting days we'd walk there, maybe play tennis and sometimes go out in one of the boats on the lake.

Sheila Dorling (née Smith)

Right: Gants Hill greetings.

Below: Roy Wilkinson, the Shining Knight.

Shining Knight

I was driving home in April 1960 when I noticed a family had broken down. I pulled over and got the car going. They were so pleased they bought me cup of tea in the café. I was in the Knights of the Road, who were a club to promote good and helpful driving. They asked about the headlight badge. The *News of the World* did something similar which the man had heard of. Anyway they took my details and wrote to the *News of the World*. On the letter that came from the paper it said 'We are glad to inform you that you have been elected by the Executive Council to be a Member of the Order of the Knights of the Road in recognition of your courtesy and care on the highway.' I got a certificate and a coat badge. I then helped another chap when his car had broken down near my house. He stood in the hallway having a cup of tea and noticed my certificate on the wall. He wrote down the details saying I had been helpful. In October 1960 they promoted me to a Companion of the Order of the Knights of the Road. I received another certificate and a car badge engraved with my membership number. On

their paperwork the aim of their order was 'To restore something of old world chivalry and kindliness to our roads in the hope that this will make for road safety. We feel that many accidents would be avoided if all road users would give thought to others and that is why we are laying such stress on the value of courtesy'.

Roy Wilkinson

Dr Findlay's boat rides

At the other end of Aldborough Road North is St Peter's church and this played a large part in the local community. My father supplied many alcoholic and soft drinks for the various weddings and social events held there. There was a yearly fête and one of the GPs, Dr Findlay, used to give people boat rides on the small lake in the grounds. The church was built from the old stones from the original Westminster Bridge.

Brenda Graisgour

To Barkingside

I was born and lived in Birkbeck Road and would travel to Barkingside by tram from the Horns tavern which terminated at the Chequers. I went to school at Perrymans Farm Road and I used to run errands and get tuppence for cleaning my brother's tennis shoes.

D. Williams

Clayhall and Claybury

There was no Clayhall estate. It was all open fields, most farmed by Claybury. On a Sunday we used to go up what we called the Boards that separated Claybury from the Barkingside side. Get over the stiles and watch the football team called the All Blacks. Further on from there was a ring of trees on a hill and that was always known as Cocked Hat Hill – because of its shape. Apart from that there were no other buildings until they built a fully furnished show bungalow forming part of the new Clayhall estate. The man that looked after it we called Gritty Whiskers. He used to

let us kids play in there. No one ever damaged anything and nothing was ever stolen. It was different from the old two-bedroomed cottages that we used to live in. Clayhall and Claybury were classed as our back garden.

Len Smith

Claybury and the Glade

We often walked up the road to the forest and spent some enjoyable afternoons in a little clearing we called the Glade. The forest seemed to be fairly extensive to me being a small child and in the summer it was carpeted with wild anemones.

Joan Medlock

Tenants' association

I was born in Ilford in 1943 and moved to Barkingside in January 1948 with my parents and older brother. It was a freezing cold winter and I remember moving into a new house on a new estate. This was very exciting for all the family as previously we had lived in an upstairs

Len Smith, 2005.

Sandra Corderoy, her brother and cousin in their garden, *c*. 1950.

West Ham Hammers speedway track next to Fairlop sailing lake, 2004.

flat. There were no pavements and all I can remember is all the mud everywhere. A tenants' association was formed and many events were organised including trips to the seaside, socials every month and Christmas parties. I celebrated my fifth birthday by having a party and inviting the neighbours and my many new friends. All of the houses were occupied by families with young children. I got my first pram and I thought it was wonderful. I already had a favourite doll which my uncle had brought me back after the war.

Sandra Corderoy (*née* Taylor)

West Ham Hammers

Where the day centre once was at Fullwell Cross was open land with a large tree in it. It once was a speedway track for bikes. Local lads would turn their bikes into speedway bikes and pedal round like mad, calling themselves the West Ham Hammers. They then acquired a piece of land from the council at the bottom of Forest Road, what is now the far end of Fairlop Waters before Hainault Road, and the whole team moved down there. I think to this day the track is still in existence.

Bert Reed

The Horns public house, David St Pierre is standing by the road.

Charlie

When I worked in Tucker's butchers a well-loved local character used to call in – Charlie the road sweeper, who kept Barkingside High Street immaculate for as many years as I can remember. He used to sweep out our shop yard in exchange for a pigs head. He was a good humoured, friendly man with a gentle Caribbean accent. I know he was dreaming of the warm sunshine and blue seas of his homeland on his retirement. Last time I saw him these plans were underway. I hope he and his wife got their wish because he certainly deserved it after his dedication and hard work in our town.

Carol Baldwin

Generations of St Pierres

My St Pierre relatives have been resident in Barkingside and the surrounding villages for several generations. My mother, Joyce St Pierre, lived with her two brothers (until her marriage in 1934) at No. 90 Horns Road, opposite the TA centre, on the same side as the Horns public house, further down were the local shops. During the Second World War both my uncles were away from the area, Roger in Burma with the Chindits and David in Gibraltar serving as a batman. All three are buried in St Peter's, Aldborough Hatch.

No. 90 Horns Road has now been demolished but it was a semi-detached house and looked from the outside as if it was built of wood. It had no gas or electricity and had an outside toilet. The lighting was with an oil lamp and candles. Heating and hot water was from a range in the kitchen. Baths were in front of this range in a tin bath with the water heated from the range. Going to bed was with the aid of a candle.

Peter Cubbidge

All Saints' church, Chigwell Row.

Milk churns

We did most of our shopping round the corner in the parade near Hamilton Avenue. Everything you needed in about six or seven shops. I remember the horse-drawn milk carts. You would take your jug to the milkman and he would ladle out a pint or two from the churn. I don't know if it was pasteurised or not. Other produce was delivered by van.

John Baker

Riding the goat

My husband played the piano in various pubs in the area, the Crooked Billet, Two Brewers and the Maypole (Chigwell Row) and in his younger days, before we met, the Retreat. It was after a night at the Retreat that he and his friends were making their way back home. One of the friends had a slight disability and was unable to walk far. There was no transport available except for the goat in nearby Trotter's field. They lifted him onto its back and strapped him on. Luckily for him, the goat seemed to know its destination because he arrived home in one piece. My husband and fellow companions tethered it on the field down at Fullwell Cross (near to where the toilets have been demolished) but in the morning it had gone. The next time they went up Chigwell Row it was happily grazing in the field.

E. Kemble

Development of Barkingside

The big year for housing development was 1934. The estate, which is the largest part of the area behind Mossford Lane incorporating most of the roads round Clayhall, was built by New Ideals Homes. But the roads behind the High Street such as Fairlop Road were built earlier, either the end of 1933 or early 1934. Some of these were built by the Hobbs family who owned the garage in the High Street.

Ron Ketteridge

Aldborough stores

Next door to Aldborough stores off-licence, which my father ran, was a newsagent's/tobacconist's called Thompson's, and across the alleyway the other side of the shop was the GP's surgery. Behind the shop was a large block of flats called Aldborough Court. All these buildings remain there today although both shops are now run more like general grocery stores.

Brenda Graisgour

Haunted house

Where Starch House Lane is was fields. We would go across, under the little arch under the railway and walk through into Aldborough Hatch. The big old house there I think was called Aldborough Hall. We would scrump apples and say it was haunted by ghosts to frighten each other.

Roy Wilkinson

King George Hospital

The new King George Hospital has been built almost opposite Happy Valley. I spent many hours at Happy Valley and was always fascinated by the area on the opposite side of the road. It always seemed too dark and mysterious to venture into. I believe it is still accessible, certainly it is gated and the flight of steps remains. I think the stream, known as Seven Kings Water, passes at the back of Seven Kings Park and emerges at Westwood Park where there was a shallow boating lake.

Geoffrey Gillon

Tomswood Hill

Where the shop still is in Tomswood Hill were two cottages. On one side Mrs Burgess had her shop in a wooden place and at the back was stables, an orchard and tennis courts. Further along were more cottages, a smallholding and then more cottages; the Chaplins lived along there as well as a couple of elderly ladies. The lane that went round the back was always known as the 'Old Blind Lane'. Not sure why it was called that but it had a bend in it. It is now Mossford Lane.

Len Smith

Sleepy Sunday

Sundays in Tomswood Hill were very quiet in the 1970s. Very few cars would pass by. Sunday dinner was important, sitting at the table as a family. A roast at lunchtime, and shellfish and crumpets for tea. In the morning I would go over to the allotment hut with my dad to get seeds and soil for the allotment he had in Mossford Lane. We spent many an hour over there planting and picking our home-grown produce. I would then be pushed back home in the wheelbarrow with all the veg on my lap.

H. Kemble

ten

Memorable Times

Keeping in touch

Having been in contact in recent years via various websites with old acquaintances and school friends, it seems that most of us have some good memories of our life within a local community.

Brenda Graisgour

No trouble

There was no trouble like there is today. The police would be on their bikes and if you wanted to know the time you would ask a policeman. If you were caught doing something wrong you would get a clip round the ear and you would be taken home. Then you would get another clip round the ear off your dad!

Bert Reed

Green crinoline

I remember King George VI's Coronation in 1937 when I was dressed up in a green crinoline dress and bonnet for the fancy dress parade in the road where my grandparents (Wright) lived.

Joan Knight (*née* Wright)

Mushroom ring and watercress

Looking up to the forest to the golf links area from round by the Hainault Oak there used to be three rings of mushrooms. One very large one and two small ones each side of it.

We would go over and pick them. It was there until the war when the Land Army girls put their tractors over it and ploughed it up. At the far end of the lake there was always a lovely bed of watercress coming from the stream until the 1960s.

Charles Ernest Winter

Victory parades and peaceful nights

In May 1945 VE Day was declared and a street party was planned. A good time was had by all. The real food rationing then started, there was so many shortages. Bread was rationed for the first time. Life went on though – at least we got some peaceful sleep. We also had a street party for VJ Day in the August of 1945. Barkingside Rec would also put on a regular flower show and Princes Fair would be held on the field opposite the Fairlop pub.

Joan Knight (*née* Wright)

Christmas pillowcase

At Christmas we would hang up a pillowcase, and you would be lucky if you got an orange, an apple, banana (but not in wartime) a few sweets and a couple of small presents. We were brought up before the war and we didn't have a lot of money. We were lucky and grateful for what we had.

Roy Wilkinson

Barkingside Recreation Ground, *c.* 1950.

Fairlop School pupils eagerly await Princess Elizabeth's visit in Fullwell Avenue, 1950. (Courtesy of the *Ilford Recorder*)

Princess Elizabeth's visit

In 1950 the Queen (then Princess Elizabeth) came to Barkingside. The whole school was marched up to Fullwell Avenue to see her and we all had flags to wave.

Alison Bush (*née* Dryborough)

Romance in Barkingside

In January 1949 a young girl, Joan, started as office junior at the dairy. At the dinner and dance we proved we were no dancers, so my sister and her boyfriend, Eric, went with Joan and I to dancing lessons at Roylance record shop in the room at the back. Friendship led to romance and we got engaged in 1951 and married in 1953. We have enjoyed over fifty years of married life and have a lovely family.

John Knight

Enever's

Sometimes we would have a surprise visit from an aunt and uncle on a Sunday. Shops would not be open, but the cockle and winkle man would drive around the streets and we would have to listen for him so as we would have something tasty for tea. If mother was caught out like this and hadn't baked a cake, my sister Jackie and I would be sent up to Grange Hill to Enever's, a small café that opened Sunday mornings. It was a tiny shop that almost looked as if a puff of wind would knock it down. Inside there were a couple of tables where the railway workers could get cups of tea. On one side there was a rack that held newspapers and a stand where there were Lyons' cakes. We always thought it was such a treat to get shop bought cakes as

we nearly always had homemade ones. There were Swiss rolls in chocolate and cream or vanilla with jam. Also small chocolate covered teacakes, Eccles cakes and jam tarts or cream sponge cakes. We chose a chocolate and cream Swiss roll and jam tarts and had to give ration stamps as well as money, because sweets and confectionery was still on ration. They also sold R. Whites lemonade or cream soda and Tizer. Behind the door as you entered the shop was a small counter and glass cabinet that held a variety of sweets, black jacks or fruit salad chews, liquorice, sherbet dabs or fountains, behind the counter were jars of sweets. Sometimes Dad would ask us to get some Woodbines for him.

Patricia Lange (*née* Dawson)

Best present ever
I remember waking up one Christmas morning and a wooden desk was by my bed – just what I wanted with pads and crayons inside it. It was the best present ever.

Sheila Dorling (*née* Smith)

Above: John and Joan Knight in Holy Trinity church, 2003.

Left: Getting ready for the VJ party.

Princess who?

I remember at school one day a Princess was to travel along Eastern Avenue towards Southend. We were all marched along to Green Gate and stood on the edge of the road to wave as she went by. I don't know who she was, but I remember it was drizzling rain.

V.E. Bush

Party memories

Every 5th November we had a big bonfire and potato roast across the road from the main gate (next to the church) of Dr Barnardo's Home, where the flats are now. I remember the fair, which used to come to Barkingside, across from and to the left of the Fairlop pub. There were rides and games. I had my first Chair O'Plane ride there. As children we would go to the aerodrome and have bicycle races. I was young when we had a VJ party for the children in 1945. These were the children that lived on Duke Road, Crown Road and Princes Road. That night the adults had a party in the streets. They had a piano, bonfire, dancing and singing. They were having a ball.

Maureen Lewis

Playground parades

We had a parade in the playground for Empire Day and a maypole on May Day. A May Queen and her attendants were dressed up and pulled round the playground in a cart decorated with flowers.

Joan Knight (*née* Wright)

Pea-souper

A pea-souper, for the many lucky souls who have never been in one, was a dense fog. Even in Barkingside we had some of them. The one I particularly remember seemed to come on very suddenly. It was a bit misty one night and, then, there it was the following morning. This was fog like you see in old films.

I used to walk to Gilbert Colvin School with my friend, Brenda, who lived across the road. I usually called for her each morning. I started across the road in the smog. I couldn't see the other side. This is a typical Barkingside residential road – it is wide enough for two cars to pass and that is all. The fog swirled so you might be in a clearish bit one moment and a really opaque bit the next. I hit an opaque bit as I crossed the road. I slowed down and was distracted by a noise. It wasn't a car, there was hardly any traffic in our road,

Princes Road and Crown Road
VJ-Day party in full swing.

but I looked around and turned a little way on one foot. Then I was lost! I could see neither side of the road. I don't mean that I couldn't see the houses on either side; I mean I could not even see the kerbs. Feeling a bit panicky, I took a direction and found it was uphill so I was going up the middle of the road. I turned sharply to one side and walked that way. I soon found a kerb by stumbling over it. Across the pavement, I found a gate with a number on it. I was back on my own even numbered side of the road. So I tried again. I walked as briskly as I dared and as straight as I could to the other side then patted my way along the fences, hedges and walls down to Brenda's house. As I recall, she and her mother were already at the door looking out into the shifting veils of murk. It was smashing. We could be late for school with a good excuse. I'm not sure if anyone was on time that day.

Roger O'Brien

Once eaten never forgotten

My best mates at school were Danny Bradley and George Reynolds, along with my neigh-bours, Brian Reading and Brian (Ginger) Morley. Most pupils stayed for school dinners, which were served in a long wooden hut on the playing field. You queued up along the narrow passageway and could smell what you were getting long before getting within sight. 'Frogspawn' or tapioca pudding along with macaroni was often served as dessert. It was stodgy and awful. Occasionally we skipped dinner and spent the money on bags of broken biscuits from the local shop opposite the school.

Ray Burton

Garden cane crinoline

For the 1953 Coronation we had a street party, but as we were on a main road we went in with Addison Road and the part of Tomswood Hill that formed the triangle. We had a great time with races, a tea, coronation cake cut by the Ilford Carnival Queen, and as it rained they managed to get hold of a marquee and erect it on the wasteland in the triangle. In the evening someone wheeled out their piano and there was dancing and singing, food and drink. All the children had a commemorative cup, saucer, plate and a medal. Every child in the borough was given a book called 'Royalty in Essex' and

Barkingside and District social outing to Clacton.

Fairlop secondary school recreated the Fairlop Fair. Each year were given an era. My year was Victorian and my mother made me a crinoline from garden cane and starched old curtains.

Alison Bush (*née* Dryborough)

Bad habits

You could buy sweet cigarettes and pretend to smoke. They banned them years ago now. We also put flour in glitter tubes so when you puffed them it looked like smoke.

Angela Bishop

Coronation television

The most memorable event for me was the Queen's Coronation. Televisions were indeed a luxury in those days and we got one not long before. A twelve-inch Bush that enabled us to watch the ceremony. A real treat.

Hazel Pudney

Manners go a long way

Our manager at Frank Norman's made sure we were polite and courteous to customers so as to keep their custom. I still see people or their children whom I served then. We had a friendly but polite relationship with them and it is nice now, over forty years later, to talk about old times. Sometimes we would give the children a broken biscuit while they were queuing to be served.

E. Kemble

Treasured book

I have a wartime cookery book. I found it at a book sale. It is a treasure that I shall pass on to my daughter. Inside this book I found notes from a vicar's wife to her cleaner telling her what work she wanted done that day. That lady was probably paid a pittance and she must have earned every penny of it. Thank goodness times have changed.

V. Payne

Second prize just won't do

One of the highlights of the year was the local flower show, held in Barkingside Recreation Ground. My father always exhibited and there was great rivalry between him and Mr

Miss Wiseman's Fairlop school fifth-form experimental class, 1957.

Wilkinson as to who took first and second place in the vegetable sections. They also had rides, sideshows, tug-of-war plus a dance show put on by a school, which was held in a hall at the back of Roylance the music shop in the High Street.

Alison Bush (*née* Dryborough)

Local chit-chat

I remember one character called Len who came from Claybury. He used to hang around outside Brett's hairdressers and the cinema. I always spoke to him and he would come out with different jobs he once had. One example that sticks in my mind was that he had cut Frank Sinatra's toenails. I also remember a couple of the local policemen would come in Brett's and have a chat. People had respect for the police then.

Ann Reed (*née* Croft)

Ann and Bert Reed in 1959.

Rural community

Barkingside was a much more rural community than now. Some of my earliest memories are of being taken to see the horses at the blacksmith's opposite the rec. From quite a young age I would go on errands to the shops at the end of the road. There were fields opposite and beyond our house where circuses, fairs and gymkhanas were held. Behind our house were prefab bases and we adopted one as a tennis court and would spend hours playing tennis or roaming out the back with the girls from two houses along, Ann and Judy. My husband too remembers playing on wasteland opposite the Boys' County High.

E. Wood

Convenient area

I still reside in Barkingside with my husband although my family has now moved out of the area. It is convenient for transport and local shops. I still see some old faces when I'm out but it isn't the same.

Rose Dean

Doughnuts

One of my favourite shops was Pither's bakery, you could smell the hot bread smells wafting down the street before you got there and we always got a treat of jam sugar doughnuts. You would bite into the sugary sticky dough and the sugar would stick to your fingers and cheeks, and with the next bite the warm jam would ooze out. They were well worth the mess you made with them. The only thing I enjoyed more was an ice cream cone at Rossi's ice-cream parlour; no other cone has ever tasted like it since.

Patricia Lange (*née* Dawson)

Trouser apples

Just before the entrance to the airfield, via a track where Aldborough Road ended, was an orchard with many apple trees. We would go scrumping there. I remember when I was fourteen I had on a pair of baggy trousers, tucked into my socks and with bicycle clips for additional security. I filled them up with apples from my ankles to my knees. Beginning to ride home on my bike with great difficulty from the bulk of the apples, I was appalled that the right trouser leg became loose and I lost a trail of apples, just as a motorcycle policeman was passing. He didn't stop but I was relieved that it wasn't my Dad, who was also a speed cop.

John Coborn

Pegging out the pounds

One memory of coming home from school one day was seeing my brother's jeans pegged on the line, together with a line of £1 notes that he had forgotten to take out of his pockets and were now drying.

Linda Reside

Red, white and blue

When it was the Queen's Silver Jubilee in 1977, my husband bedded our garden out in red, white and blue. We didn't have a street party as we lived on a main road but we had bunting at the front of our house and many of the other houses were decorated. Lots of the smaller turnings nearby had parties as they had to get permission to shut the roads. My daughter was given a bookmark at school, presented by the London Borough of Redbridge to commemorate the jubilee, which she still has.

E. Kemble

Covered in pig

I was training to be a plumber and did a bit of work for Albany so used to hang around down there with the older lads from the village. I remember a friend, Tommy Hadlam, who was a lighterman down at Millwall Docks and he got a pig once and took it down Albany's on Saturday morning – they were going to share it out. They suggested it was cut up on the circular saw so someone, whose name escapes me, started cutting it and the whole place ended up with bits of pig all over the place. We were all covered. I was just the onlooker.

Bert Reed

I'm stuck

In the biology class we had these horrible tall stools and they had three rungs on them to put your feet. The seats weren't very big and they had a hole in the centre where you could pick them up. I did this one day and my hand got stuck. That was a kafuffle trying to get my hand out.

Linda Reside

Barnardo's Christmas

Christmas at Barnardo's was wonderful because so many people gave toys to the children. There just wasn't room in the cupboards to put them all. American airmen who were billeted nearby would turn up with sack loads of toys, so Christmas for the children was lovely. We always had a church service at the church in the grounds.

Kathy Alston

Karl-Heinz Rüping

It was in 1973 when we were living in Greenwood Gardens that I returned home one day to be told that some Germans had come looking for me. Apparently they had

Left: Dr Barnardo's statue. (Courtesy of Barnardo's)

Below: Karl-Heinz Rüpeng at Fairlop POW camp.

during the war years when he was a prisoner at Fairlop and for the coat I had given him, he wanted to find me again. It was an emotional reunion. We kept in touch and one day he called to ask what holiday plans we had. He invited us to spend a holiday with him and his family. We had a very interesting and happy time. Unfortunately he died a couple of years ago. We still keep in touch with his family. It was a long-term friendship that never died.

Charles Ernest Winter

Knees up Mother Brown

VE Day was celebrated in Merlin Grove. I took my cup and plate and sat at a table as long as the road. The adults were very cheerful, dancing the Hokey-Cokey and Knees up Mother Brown.

Pat Owers

tried on many trips to England but were amazed how many 'C. Winters' there were in the phonebook. Luckily they had left details of the hotel where they were staying in Ilford. I couldn't believe it when I saw Karl-Heinz. He had been so grateful for my friendship

Apple Pie Ingram

A.P. Ingram was a local builder. Being kids we used to raid his apple trees. He lived opposite us in the High Street, in the big house on the corner of Baron Gardens. He caught us scrumping and made us sit there and eat these green apples until we complained of stomach ache. He said then perhaps wouldn't do it again. We also got a cuff up the back of the ear and told that he would tell mother when he saw her.

When I was married I was working over George E. Grays when this van came in. The bloke got out and cuffed me up the back of the head. 'I know you; you're Annie Smith's son'. After all those years he remembered. Because of his initials we called him Apple Pie.

Len Smith

The King is dead

When I was in the juniors I remember being told on 6 February 1952 that the King had died and I felt very sad. My father bought a black and white television set just before the Coronation in June of that year and the neighbours came in to watch. Compared with today the screen was small, about nine inches, but the box was enormous. My Mum stayed behind with my brother, cousin and me whilst my father, aunt and uncle actually went up to the Mall in London to watch the procession. They camped out overnight in order to get a good view. We were very patriotic waving our flags at the television set. I was even dressed in red shorts, white blouse and a blue cardigan.

Sandra Corderoy (*née* Taylor)

Above: William Ingram's Pert Cottages sign – relative of A.P. Ingram.

Right: Pert Cottages have retained their original look.

Fairlop school, Mr Garratt's class, c. 1954.

Wedding photograph of Charles and Doris Winter.

Greenwood Gardens

Living in Greenwood Gardens was pleasant. We spent a good few years there bringing up our family of six children. Whilst there we had a VE Day street party to celebrate the fifty years.

Doris Winter

Famous faces

Sally Gunnell's dad sometimes visited Fairlop school fêtes with his donkeys for the children to ride. He had a farm in nearby Chigwell.

Ray Ross

Dad, Duffle Coat and the Barkingside Mob

I remember when I was fourteen going over the Barkingside end of the airfield with a bunch of about six kids. We happened to meet up with another bunch of kids – apparently it was their territory and someone started throwing stones. It must have been winter as I was wearing a brand new duffle coat, which I had been pestering my father to buy me for some time (these were all the rage in that era). There was a row of 'tank traps' at each end of the bridge. Each gang was behind these blocks throwing stones

Charles and Doris Winter, 2005.

across the no-man's land. I, stupidly, picked up a large conglomeration of bricks, still cemented together and probably part of a demolished or bomb-damaged building, ran across the dividing line and lobbed it over the tank trap behind which I suspected there was one of the enemy lurking. There was a loud scream of pain from behind the block and we all knew that some kind of serious injury had occurred. As one we decided to scarper. We ran down into the area beneath the bridge. I took off my new coat while running for fear of falling. I rolled it up and fell anyway, sliding several yards down the slope on top of my coat. It was totally ingrained with mud. In desperation I went to the water and tried to wash the mud off. I managed to get most of it out but in doing so removed the soft pile from the surface. I went home with my damaged coat hoping my father (who was very strict) wouldn't notice. He did, however, and I got a good hiding.

John Coborn

Famous Faces II

I vacuumed around Trevor Brooking's feet one day whilst working in Fags 'n' Mags in Barkingside. I did not even realise who he was. Bobby Moore would often jog past our house as he lived just off Tomswood Hill and Pat Jennings also popped in to buy the odd newspaper.

Amanda Ross

Luck Duck and Vanish

The worst bomb that I remember was at the Bald Hind hill on the Prince of Wales pub. There was a darts match taking place the night the land mine hit. It killed a lot of local people. Opposite was the Hainault telephone exchange – they used to put a sort of Home Guard there (LDV – Luck Duck and Vanish they used to call them). They used to stand them on duty. On this particular day this bloke stood at attention with his rifle by his side. The police kept asking him if he had seen anything and he was just standing there, he wasn't hurt or anything. I suppose it was the blast and shock that had killed him.

Roy Wilkinson

Losing the conveniences

It is an inconvenience that the toilets at Fullwell Cross have been knocked down to make way for flats. They were very useful when out shopping or coming back from the school.

Marjorie Ketteridge

Table top op

When I was about seven I had to have a minor operation. My parents didn't like me going to hospital so they arranged for it to be done at home on the dining room table. It would never have been allowed nowadays. It was quite expensive for my parents to have this done. They sold all their national savings certificates they had built up for me to pay for it.

John Baker

Hula-hula girl

In June 1953, when I was seven years old, everybody had street parties and there was a record out at the time by Guy Mitchell called 'She wears red feathers and a hula-hula skirt'. So my Mum, Dad and aunt who lived round

John and Mary Baker's wedding.

the corner decided that I would be a hula-hula girl. They made me this grass skirt and to make me look darker they used ordinary cold cream and cocoa powder and mixed it together, then this concoction was plastered all over me. It was awful. I had this rose in my hair and we all had to line up so that we could be judged. It was so cold that I had put a cardigan on as I didn't have anything on my top and 1953 wasn't a very warm year, I might add. My brother was fifteen and he was a sea cadet, part of the RMVR. He had his navy suit and was dressed as a sailor. The lad across the road was a spiv, a moustache, trilby and a big kipper tie; others were dressed as Andy Pandy, different pirates, sailors and all sorts like that. Unfortunately I didn't win a prize because I didn't stand still long enough. We had games at the street party, food on trestle tables, streamers and flags. Things were still on ration so food was limited.

Linda Reside

King of the Co-op Empire

Opposite the Chequers pub in the High Street stood a small complex of Co-op shops. There was a small supermarket, butcher's and greengrocer's. Aged fourteen, I approached the manager, Mr Sid Elmore, and asked if there were any vacancies for a Saturday boy. Right time, right place. After speaking to my mum, he agreed that I could start the following week. My pay? Nineteen shillings and sixpence a week. My job? Cleaning, shelf-filling, delivering boxes of groceries, keeping the warehouse and yard tidy.

There was no delivery bike so I had to walk the boxes of groceries round (just after lunch) on a sack barrow. My Saturday walk extremes took me to houses in Fencepiece Road, Caterham Avenue, Bute Road and Campbell Avenue, with other stops in between. I worked there for three years. By the end I had learned how to bone a side of bacon, helped cash up the cigarette kiosk, served sometimes on the bacon counter

Co-op Society Ltd, Barkingside High Street, in the 1950s.

and was responsible for adding items to the weekly tinned food warehouse order. My wages had risen to twenty-five shillings a week.

The final summer I was busying in the warehouse when Sid Elmore found me and told me that Mr King the area manager wanted to talk to me. Was I in trouble? I had been recommended by Sid Elmore to take on a role as relief around the local Co-op Empire also if I did well in my A' levels, there was a place for me as a trainee manager. I'd made it – in Co-op terms!

Whilst learning life-embellishing skills such as how to bone a side of bacon, I also went out with Kay, the daughter of the chief bacon saleslady, for three years. What a lot I gained from the Co-op!

Derek Lawrence

Bus-stop gnomes

I always remember the garden full of gnomes by the bus stop at the Maypole pub in Fencepiece Road.

Angela Bishop

Nissan hut tennis

When they took the huts down they left the bases. We taught our daughters to play tennis on them. We had a gate at the back of the garden and would have bonfire parties out there with the Turner family who lived along the road. Mums would bring sausages and things like that and we would have a real party. All the five houses in our row had young children.

Ron Ketteridge

Other local titles published by Tempus

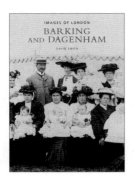

Barking and Dagenham
GAVIN SMITH

Barking and Dagenham have been sister communities on the Thames shore from Saxon times, but the modern communities we know today began to take shape with the arrival of the Ford Company and the rapid growth of its manufacturing plant at Dagenham. This collection of old photographs illustrates many of the changes that have taken place and will appeal to all who live and work in the area.

0 7524 0739 2

Memories of Epping
CLARE BASTER

The market town of Epping has seen much expansion and a great many changes in its long history. Recollections of times past are recorded here along with over 100 archive photographs, many from private and unique collections. *Memories of Epping* will take the reader on a nostalgic journey into the past of this fascinating part of Essex and will delight all those who want to know more about the area.

0 7524 3453 5

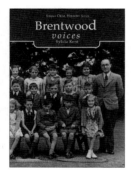

Brentwood Voices
SYLVIA KENT

This fascinating compilation of reminiscences records life in Brentwood, a town once described as a tiny hamlet on the Great Essex Road but now an expanding borough with a growing population. The personal stories recall childhood, work and family, war and peace, and the pastimes of previous generations. Illustrated with a wide selection of photographs, this book offers a nostalgic glimpse into Brentwood's past.

0 7524 2247 2

Essex Thames-side: Woolwich to Thorpe Bay
CHRIS THURMAN

Chris Thurman takes the reader on a tour of the Thames from Woolwich to Thorpe Bay on the Essex side of the river. From the futuristic sight of the Thames Barrier to sleepy Thorpe Bay, from unloading in the docks at Tilbury to cockling at Leigh on Sea, from Dagenham to Southend, the changing landscape of Essex Thames-side is photographed over the past forty years in this stunning collection of images.

0 7524 3232 X

If you are interested in purchasing other books published by Tempus, or in case you have difficulty finding any Tempus books in your local bookshop, you can also place orders directly through our website

www.tempus-publishing.com